EXETER STUDIES IN HISTORY

General Editor

C.D.H.Jones   BA DPhil FRHistS

Editorial Committee

M.Duffy   MA DPhil FRHistS
R.H.Higham BA PhD

M.D.D.Newitt   BA PhD FRHistS
I.A.Roots   MA FSA FRHistS

ISBN 0 85989 238 7

ISSN 0260 8626

Printed and bound in Great Britain by Short Run Press Ltd., Exeter.

Contents

List of Figures

Preface

This volume contains four lectures which were given in Exeter between 15 October and 5 November 1986 in association with an exhibition, <u>Domesday Devon</u>, held in the Cathedral Library from 14 to 30 October 1986. When it was decided to mark locally the 900th anniversary of Domesday Book, it was thought appropriate to arrange lectures by scholars who had close associations with the University of Exeter. Although, consequently, not all aspects of Domesday are covered here, the volume does have a noticeably south-western flavour which should appeal to those interested in medieval Devon as well as to all those interested in the great survey and in the times in which it was made. We have also thought it valuable to include an essay describing the contents of the exhibition, and setting the survey within the wider context of the archaeological and physical record.

It was a good augury for the success of this venture when the Dean and Chapter of the Cathedral agreed to sponsor the lectures and the exhibition, and we are most grateful for their share in them. Three of the lectures took place, with their permission, in the Chapter House, and therefore close to the exhibition.

Warm thanks are due to the cartographers in the Department of Geography of the University who drew the maps, and to Seán Goddard, who designed the poster for the exhibition, and the cover of this volume.

Christopher Holdsworth

Domesday Book 1086-1986

DAVID BATES

In 1986 Domesday Book has an awesome reputation. Indeed it seems to
have had one throughout the nine centuries of its existence. In the
very year in which it was made the anonymous writer of the Anglo-Saxon
Chronicle described the collection of the material in awestruck and
shocked words.(1) It was certainly much venerated in the 1170s when
Richard fitz Nigel in the Dialogue of the Exchequer first mentioned the
name under which the record is known:

> This book is metaphorically called by the native
> English Domesday, that is the Day of Judgement.
> For as the sentence of that strict and terrible
> last account cannot be evaded by any subterfuge,
> so when this book is appealed to on those matters
> which it contains, its sentence cannot be quashed
> or set aside with impunity.(2)

These references are just the beginning of a long sequence which cover
the nine hundred years of Domesday Book's existence and which show that
profound respect for the survey, its contents and its administrative
value are in general normal.

High expectations have also characterised academic study of
Domesday Book, which has been carried on with increasing intensity for
about three hundred years. One measure of this is the 1757 entries
included in the Domesday Bibliography which I have published for the
Royal Historical Society.(3) Another is the belief that if we could
only understand Domesday Book, then the mists of the first one thousand
years of English history might be cleared. F. W. Maitland's Preface to
his Domesday Book and Beyond states the ideal:

> I have followed that retrogressive method 'from
> the known to the unknown', of which Mr Seebohm is
> the apostle. Domesday Book appears to me, not
> indeed as the known, but as the knowable. Beyond
> is still very dark: but the way to it lies
> through the Norman record.(4)

Domesday Book's supposed accuracy and comprehensivenesss is therefore something of a trap. Surprise that it is not an infallible source of information has, in consequence, been expressed by those disappointed not to discover what they expected. The example which most readily springs to mind is Samuel Pepys' enquiry about what Domesday Book said about the sea. He subsequently wrote that Domesday Book 'appears contrary to the perpetual and vulgar appreciation of it, to be no true general survey of England, but a very imperfect one'.(5) More poignantly, the list of those who have gone to law in the confidence that William the Conqueror's great survey would help them and have been disappointed is a very long one indeed. To my mind the saddest cases are those of the fourteenth-century peasants who had the record consulted in disputes over services to their lords and who lost their cases.

In similar vein modern academic study has taken us a long way towards understanding Domesday Book's limitations. The severest critics have been scholars who have questioned its administrative value and doubted whether it could have been used in the eleventh century: 'an inestimable boon to learned posterity, but a vast administrative mistake'.(6) Although all serious students of the survey now see it as an imperfect and limited record, few would go to such extremes. Maitland's methodology is still being used to great profit.(7) But some of the burden of expectation is being taken away by archaeologists who are adding to the corpus of knowledge for the dark period before 1086. They are helping to illuminate Domesday Book from beyond. And in the use of the computer, there are possibilities that earlier generations never thought of. Useful results are already being produced.(8)

As the result of a most valuable book recently published by Dr Elizabeth Hallam, we can know to a very full extent the way in which Domesday Book has been used over the centuries. Her search in the central records at the Public Record Office and in the printed sources has been massive and she has undoubtedly established the clear outlines of Domesday Book's history. Fresh evidence is likely to come only from unpublished local records and many uncertainties about the whole subject have been laid to rest.(9) The book's sustained theme is Domesday Book's continuous nine-hundred-year living history. The survey was a legal record consulted throughout the Middle Ages and the early modern period and is still admissible as evidence in court. It has been consulted for practical purposes in the twentieth century, as, for example, in a famous case in the House of Lords in 1902 to determine who should hold the title of Lord Great Chamberlain.(10) We are also given a survey of the way in which the record has been kept, published and used by historians and antiquaries.

Domesday Book proper, that is, the two volumes known as Great Domesday and Little Domesday, was first published in 1783. The editor was Abraham Farley and the two volumes have an entirely justified reputation for accuracy. Two further volumes, containing an introduction by Sir Henry Ellis, indexes, and the texts of the two 'satellites', <u>Exon</u> Domesday Book and the <u>Inquisitio Eliensis</u>, as well as two other surveys, <u>Liber Winton</u> and Boldon Book, were published in 1816 and issued in 1817.(11) A photozincographic facsimile was made between 1861 and 1864 by the Ordnance Survey Office at Southampton and translations included in the relevant volume of the <u>Victoria County Histories of England</u>.(12) In 1986 Domesday Book is much more accessible than ever before. The Phillimore edition, begun in 1975, is now complete. This is an invaluable publication, despite the spurious modernity of its translation of technical terms. Now Alecto Historical Editions have produced a sumptuous facsimile of the whole text, with separate county volumes compiled under the general editorship of Dr Ann Williams.

The modern study of Domesday Book is usually thought to begin with the 1886 Commemoration, the voluminous publications of John Horace Round, and Maitland's <u>Domesday Book and Beyond</u>. This is in large degree correct. Round's contribution was a massive one which set out many of the principles on which modern Domesday scholarship is based. Maitland, a master of synthesis in a way which Round was not, offered a sweeping survey of English society and a prophetic vision of the way in which Domesday Book could be used. Bibliographical research suggests, however, that the true take-off came in the 1850s and 1860s, the era when many county journals came into existence; the Reverend William Eyton was undoubtedly the most important Domesday scholar of this period, while Hamilton's publication in 1876 of <u>Inquisitio Comitatus Cantabrigiensis</u> was a massive stimulus to Round's work. Nonetheless, even earlier work can contain some remarkable anticipations of later theories. The use of maps may seem a very modern technique, yet some Domesday churches were most effectively mapped in 1787 by Samuel Denne to show that the Domesday record of churches is incomplete. (13) Even more strikingly, the view that <u>Exon</u> was the source of the Exchequer volume, which we in the twentieth century associate with F. H. Baring and V. H. Galbraith, was first propounded in a paper given to the Society of Antiquaries by Dr Lyttleton, dean of Exeter, in 1756. A text of this paper has recently been acquired by Exeter Cathedral Library.(14) Eyton suggested that 'they (the commissioners) seem to have had at their command Territorial Records, more or less full and exact, of several periods of the Confessor's reign, if not of still earlier date'.(15) Dr Sally Harvey, with much more convincing documentation, has argued the same case since the early 1970s.

Domesday studies have developed and expanded since 1886. The great survey has been attacked through the various new academic disciplines of the twentieth century. After Round and Maitland the 1920s and 1930s look to be the crucial decade, for it was then that D. C. Douglas and, devastatingly, V. H. Galbraith began to develop new ideas on how Domesday Book was made, and in the 1930s that H. C. Darby and his early collaborators first began systematically to map the information in Domesday. After Galbraith the history of Domesday Book as an administrative document could never be the same again. Professor Darby's immense task was not complete until 1977. At the same time, R. V. Lennard began to show what an economic historian could accomplish with Domesday Book. Alongside these advances, the most basic work of all, the identification of the Domesday place-names, has continued unobtrusively. Sir William Dugdale made what is probably the first serious attempt to do this in his Antiquities of Warwickshire published in 1656. H. C. Darby's and G. R. Versey's Domesday Gazeteer, which appeared in 1975, has the appearance of a comprehensive survey of the place-names. Valuable as it is, it suffers from not discussing controversial identifications. And fresh identifications have been made during the last ten years, most notably in the Phillimore volumes edited by Frank and Caroline Thorn.(16) The sub-tenants of Domesday Book await their gazeteer. In this field major discoveries can still be made, as by Dr David Crouch, who has convincingly identified Roger de Beaumont as a sub-tenant with extensive holdings on the fief of bishop Odo of Bayeux.(17)

In trying to comment on the history of Domesday Book from 1086 to 1986, it is salutary to reflect how uncertain we still are about the processes by which Domesday Book was made and the motives for which it was made. Modern thinking has passed through three main stages. Relying heavily on the Inquisitio Comitatus Cantabrigiensis Round believed that the information was collected hundred by hundred and that it was rearranged into its final feudal order at Winchester.(18) Maitland, who followed Round in these matters, narrowed the motive down to a single fiscal purpose, the assessment of the geld.(19) This superseded an earlier view to which modern scholars have returned, that Domesday Book was made to provide William I with a thorough knowledge of his kingdom, of which the assessment of the geld was only a part.(20)

By bringing Exon into the discussion, Galbraith demonstrated that the intention had been to arrange the material by landowner from the beginning.(21) This simplified the administrative process since it removed the need to think that the material was rearranged between its collection by the commissioners and the final draft. But it opened up a lot of questions about the commissioners' procedures in the localities as well as giving the landowners a role in collecting the information, a point previously made by Charles Johnson and D. C. Douglas.(22) It also destroyed the direct relationship between Domesday Book and the geld, since the neat five-hide units of which Round had made so much in the Inquisitio Comitatus Cantabrigiensis were no longer visible. For Galbraith, who denied that Domesday Book had any fiscal purpose, it was 'a blue-print for feudal relations in England'.(23)

Dr Sally Harvey, accepting Galbraith's general theories, has taken understanding further forward by drawing attention to the significance of geld lists, some of them from Edward the Confessor's reign, as the basis for the ordering of the Domesday material.(24) This break-through has established a framework around which the survey could have been made, but it needs emphasis that administratively there remained a massive amount of work for the commissioners and the hundred jurors to do; Dr David Roffe, for example, has recently shown how vital for the final version of Domesday Book was the information from the men of the hundred in Lincolnshire.(25) It is a theory which also leaves open the question of whether the making of Domesday Book relied principally on Anglo-Saxon administrative machinery, or whether it was the culmination of Norman administrative reform. The latter view is more plausible; the introduction of the new Norman landowners must have required the revision of many tax lists, as, for example, the one behind the list of the Kent estates of bishop Odo of Bayeux in the Domesday Monachorum of Christ Church, Canterbury.(26)

Dr Harvey has also widened the scope of the motives for making the survey. She suggests an interest in the geld, in the general resources of the kingdom and in the problem of disputed title to land as a result of the Norman settlement.(27) Of particular interest is her suggestion that the ploughland statistics represent an attempt to reassess the geld.(28) This argument needs to take full account of the Norman charter evidence where all the typical Domesday Book phrases occur. It is at least obvious that, whatever its origins, the Norman terra unius carruce was more than a measure of arable capacity, since it could also refer to woodland.(29) It is also important that in Henry I's reign the geld was apparently taken on the Domesday Book hidage assessments, not on the ploughlands.(30) It could be that the new scheme was impracticable. Alternatively the reference in the Anglo-Saxon Chronicle to 'unjust gelds' taken during William Rufus's reign could indicate attempts to extend geld liability through the ploughland statistics as well as on to manorial demesne.(31) Both would have been abandoned through Henry I's Coronation Charter.(32) Local research can still tell us a lot more about the making of Domesday Book. And new developments are still possible, as, for example, in the recent demonstration that Exon Domesday Book is the direct source of the Exchequer text.(33)

For the Middle Ages after 1086 Domesday Book continued to have an administrative importance and to be used above all in legal cases. References to its use during its first century are sparse, but so too, relatively speaking, are records which can provide information about its use. The references seem to me to be numerous enough for us to be certain that it was a working document which was regularly used; just indeed what Richard fitz Nigel tells us. In c.1100, for example, an abbreviation of it was in use at Worcester.(34) Much more spectacularly, there is the Herefordshire Domesday of the 1160s, a copy of high quality of the Herefordshire folios made in the Exchequer and intended, to judge by the marginal annotations, to bring the record up to date.(35) What stands out in Dr Hallam's survey of the later consultations of Domesday Book is that procedurally it was the normal starting-point for all enquiries into rights and tenures. Exchequer officials would indeed castigate Chancery scribes if their writs failed to ask specifically for an examination of Domesday Book. Time made little difference to this process: 'in 1700 Domesday's evidence could still be called up by much the same means as in 1300 in the hope of resolving broadly similar kinds of cases'.(36)

The best known and most specialised medieval legal use of Domesday Book was in connection with cases of ancient demesne, which were concerned with the special privileges enjoyed by peasants on estates which could be shown to have been royal demesne of Edward the Confessor and William the Conqueror. Such cases continued to be heard regularly up until 1833 and ancient demesne remains an admissible plea at law.(37) The problem of origins is one not as yet fully resolved by the legal historians. It seems to me less likely that ancient demesne arose directly from economic causes and legal changes in the thirteenth century, than from the fact that from the Conquest, and before, kings had possessed special rights of exploitation over their own lands. Cases could turn on a manor's status as royal demesne long before the concept of ancient demesne had been formulated.(38) The emergence of defined procedures within an established structural framework, which is how we now view the so-called 'Angevin Leap-Forward', seems generally appropriate here too.(39)

The first recognisable Domesday Book scholars, that is men who tried seriously to understand and elucidate the text were Arthur Agarde and Robert Brady. Agarde, who was a Deputy Chamberlain of the Exchequer from 1570 to 1615 and in modern language a distinguished archivist, was for many years the custodian of Domesday Book. He worked extensively on its contents, sharing his knowledge with contemporaries such as Sir Henry Spelman and Sir Robert Cotton. He was deeply interested in the measurements and terminology of Domesday Book, he produced the first guide to its contents and made numerous annotations on the actual folios of the survey.(40) The high Tory Sir Robert Brady was another seventeenth-century historian who knew Domesday Book extremely well, making extensive use of it in his Complete History of England, published in 1685.(41) A further piece of interesting work carried out in the seventeenth century was Sir Matthew Hale's estimate of the population of Gloucestershire in 1086, the first and very precocious example of this type of interpretation.(42) It must be emphasised that these men and others worked at a time when access to Domesday Book was both difficult and costly. In 1626, for example, it cost 6/8d. to consult it and 4d. for the transcription of a single line.(43) The chest in which the two volumes were then stored survives.

The publication of Farley's edition in 1783 made a considerable difference to Domesday Book studies, although as mentioned before, the great increase in the number of publications does not come until the 1860s. Sir Henry Ellis's indexes, published in their final form in 1833 with his General Introduction to Domesday Book, remain indispensable, however, to all serious Domesday Book scholarship. They will only be superseded when the computerised indexes now being prepared are available. Important local work was done in the 1860s and 1870s, with the Reverend William Eyton's books on Staffordshire, Shropshire, Dorset and Somerset being especially notable. Eyton believed that an analysis of the statistics of Domesday Book would yield the key to the landscape and society behind the figures. His belief that the size and area of the Domesday manors could be deduced from the figures in the survey was so severely criticised by Round that he is apt to be dismissed too quickly.(44) His voluminous statistics and the reasoning which supported them seem now to belong to a world which Round and Maitland blew apart with devastating effect. He was wrong on the compilation of

Exon and he tried to assign an exact acreage to the ploughland. But he also pushed hard the view that the hide was an assessment unrelated to actual area, he accomplished fundamental work on the south-western hundreds, he suggested that geld lists assisted the ordering of the Domesday material, and he made many valuable identifications.

The massive achievements of Round and Maitland have been much written about. Round has more entries in the Domesday Bibliography than any other scholar, ninety-five to be precise. By exploiting the Inquisitio Comitatus Cantabrigiensis he showed that the way to understand the making of Domesday Book was through an analysis of its relationship with the so-called 'satellite' texts. His omission of Exon from his discussion has attracted notoriety; the use of only two 'satellites', Inquisitio Comitatus Cantabrigiensis and Inquisitio Eliensis was of course contrary to the rigorous methodology which Round himself propounded. He also established once and for all the modern view that the hide was a unit of assessment and he traced from Inquisitio Comitatus Cantabrigiensis the vast artificial system of hidation built around units of five. Characteristically Round remarked of his discovery, 'this view is so revolutionary, so subversive of all that has ever been written on the subject'.(45) Round contributed mightily to the early Victoria County Histories, writing in all thirteen Domesday Book introductions, contributing to those pioneer volumes in innumerable ways and using his Domesday introductions as vehicles for material and ideas which remain indispensable to modern work.(46) The introduction to VCH Essex is a masterpiece. That to VCH Northamptonshire included the first major study of the complex problems of that county's hidation. And he appears in several of the County journals, correcting some hapless writer who had erred.

Maitland was a gentler man, but a marvellously learned one. Whereas with Round we marvel at the knowledge and the ruthless powers of intellectual dissection, with Maitland it is the range of vision and the capacity to synthesise. Maitland's goal was to explain the origins of English society, a subject on which he belonged to the Germanist school who believed in a society of free peasants which was gradually subjected to the powers of lordship and to manorialism. He wrote in reaction to earlier work by Seebohm. On many matters Maitland's conclusions have subsequently been rejected. Tait's famous review disposed of most of the aspects of the idea that the manor of Domesday Book was a residence against which geld was assessed. He also disposed of the theory of the military origin of the English borough.(47) Later work has dealt harshly with Maitland's arguments for a universal hide of one hundred and twenty acres and on private jurisdiction in Anglo-Saxon society, as well as the general theories of the Germanists.(48) Nonetheless, to open Domesday Book and Beyond is still to wonder at the range of material which Maitland could command and at his awareness of possible future lines of enquiry. He used the statistics in Domesday Book with a sureness which none of his contemporaries could match; he showed just how treacherous the figures are, yet it is also invigorating to see his calculations confirmed by the computer.(49)

Domesday Book and Beyond and the writings of Round and Paul Vinogradoff were the basis from which a whole generation started its work. Mary Bateson, Maitland's pupil, accomplished a great deal on boroughs. Stenton and Douglas tackled the Danelaw, Tait finally produced his magisterial work on the boroughs in 1936, and Lennard published many important articles which culminated in his great work, Rural England, which appeared in 1957. Stenton developed into an outstanding scholar able in the Maitland manner to approach Domesday Book from the Anglo-Saxon side and through a superb knowledge of the later charters. Douglas did valuable work on the 'satellites', editing texts and making them available to others. Tait was a formidably sure scholar. He had also to be a controversialist, refuting the theories of the American Carl Stephenson who saw the Norman Conquest as a major turning-point in the history of English towns. Stephenson, like many vanquished in controversy, is in some danger of neglect; he was in fact a knowledgeable Domesday scholar with much to say on commendation, the making of the Domesday text, and revenues. Lennard was primarily an economic historian who wrote a series of articles on the size of peasant holdings. I am surely not alone in having found his chapter 'An Old Country' inspiring reading. His chapters on firma and estate management broke new ground.

H. C. Darby's monumental Domesday Geography also acknowledged a debt to Maitland. As the latter said:

> ... the substance of Domesday Book will have been
> rearranged. Those villages and hundreds which
> the Norman clerks tore into shreds will have been
> reconstituted and pictured in maps, for many men
> over all England will have come within King
> William's spell....(50)

Darby himself has remarked that if he had known that a project begun in the 1930s would only be completed in 1977, then his heart might have failed him.(51) The start was a paper on the Domesday woodland of East Anglia, which itself evolved from work on the Fenland.(52) Over time five regional volumes have been produced by Professor Darby and his collaborators. The last volume of the series, Domesday England, contains a valuable and moving account of the history of the whole project, saying a little - much more could be said - about the problems of making the maps and using the statistics.(53) The format of the series was to proceed on a county-by-county basis, sticking throughout to a rigid scheme. Darby himself has expressed some regrets: 'Were we to start all over again, we would probably do so on the basis of the Domesday counties', as opposed to the pre-1974 ones.(54) Values of estates were treated in some of the early articles, but then only reintroduced in the general volume which concluded the series. There will always be further clarification of the maps from intensive local work, such as has been done on the Forest of Arden in Warwickshire.(55)

While the Domesday Geography volumes were being published, a new and rewarding approach to Domesday Book was starting to develop. The Domesday Geography is a snap-shot of England in 1086, or at most of England from 1066 to 1086. Treatment is controlled by the information in Domesday Book; the series is 'a geography of Domesday Book'.(56) Intellectually it has always been thought possible to approach Domesday Book from the landscape, as from another historical source, rather than the other way round. But the major study which began the flood was W. G. Hoskins's study of settlement on the fringes of Dartmoor, which appeared in the 1960s.(57) Nowadays an increasing number of studies are stressing how unreliable Domesday Book can be as an index of settlement. At the heart of this is the contention that the apparently neat record of nucleated settlements in fact conceals a pattern in which the hamlet and the isolated farm were much more common than previously thought.(58) A point which follows is that Domesday Book, as has long been known, omits many places in existence in 1086. The inter-action of the Domesday statistics and the history of landscape is telling us a great deal about the material entered in Domesday Book. In general, archaeologists can do much to illuminate the text. Deddington (Oxfordshire), for example, has always looked to be an interesting manor because of its large demesne. Excavation of the castle site has now led to the suggestion that it may be one of the three or four main residences of bishop Odo of Bayeux.(59)

In 1986 the celebration of the nine-hundredth anniversary of the making of Domesday Book will be an international affair and will stimulate tourism. Yet study of the survey has always been something of an insular affair. It is 'our earliest public record', a survey unrivalled elsewhere for its date. We have only recently begun to discuss the possibility that it may owe something to Roman and Carolingian administration.(60) Most serious work has inevitably been undertaken within the British Isles, although there have been notable American contributions. The forthcoming Domesday Book data-base, prepared at the University of Santa Barbara, California, by Dr Robin Fleming and Dr Kathryn Mack under the supervision of Professor Warren Hollister will be invaluable for all future work. The Normans, surprisingly, have shown little interest. Serious contributions to Domesday scholarship as good as began and ended with A. L. Léchaudé d'Anisy in the nineteenth century who began a massive work intended to describe the Norman origins and the later histories of the Anglo-Norman and French families mentioned in Domesday Book. Only one volume, that containing the letter A, was ever published.(61)

Domesday studies remain vital and interesting in 1986. In the course of the past year there has been an attempt to re-define one of its most frequently used terms, the ploughland, and the nature of the sokemen remains a lively topic of discussion. Studies continue to be made which set the Domesday evidence in a wider context, with exceptionally profitable results; it is, for instance, now suggested that England was a relatively light wooded country in 1086 and that the shift away from demesne-farming which we regard as a feature of the twelfth-century economy was already well-established then.(62) In looking to the future, it is salutary to remember that the Domesday Geography project took over forty years to complete. Domesday is a complex record and there have been only a small number of truly great Domesday scholars. The record takes so long for an individual to master; most of us can only dabble. The use of computers should make a vast difference, although programming could become as demanding as the study of the record itself. The publication of a full facsimile will inevitably assist the study of the manuscript, a task which has been undertaken only since the rebinding of 1954; I would guess that Round and Maitland never looked at the manuscript except as an exhibit.(63) Another healthy influence might turn out to be the Local Government reform of 1974. It is to be hoped either that the new counties will so disrupt thinking that scholars will spend less time studying Domesday Book on a county basis, or that some other influence will push them in this direction. So much can be learnt by looking across county boundaries. On this theme, a feudal geography would be immensely valuable, to show not just the evidence for continuity and change over 1066, but also the dynamics of the Norman settlement.(64)

Notes

1. The Anglo-Saxon Chronicle, ed. D.Whitelock, with D.C.Douglas and S.I.Tucker (London, 1961), 'E', 1085.

2. Dialogus de Scaccario: The Course of the Exchequer, ed. C.Johnson, with corrections by F.E.L.Carter and D.E.Greenway (Oxford, 1983), 64.

3. D.Bates, A Bibliography of Domesday Book (Woodbridge, 1986).

4. F.W.Maitland, Domesday Book and Beyond (Cambridge, 1897), v.

5. On the Pepys' episode, see now E.M.Hallam, Domesday Book through nine centuries (London, 1986), 122.

6. H.G.Richardson and G.O.Sayles, The Governance of Medieval England from the Conquest to Magna Carta (Edinburgh, 1963), 28.

7. See, for recent examples, J.Blair, 'Secular minsters in Domesday Book', in P.Sawyer (ed.), Domesday Book: a reassessment (London, 1985), 104-42, with reference to minsters and the Viking attacks; also, R.Fleming, 'Monastic lands and England's defence in the Viking Age', EHR, 100 (1985), 247-65, for royal demesne and church lands.

8. See, for example, J.McDonald and G.D.Snooks, 'Were the Tax Assessments of Domesday Book artificial? The Case of Essex', EcHR, 2nd. series, 38 (1985), 352-72; and 'The Determinants of Manorial Income in Domesday England: Evidence from Essex', JEcH, 45 (1985), 541-56. See for a general discussion, J.Palmer, 'Domesday Book and the Computer', in Sawyer, DB, a Reassessment, 164-74.

9. Above, note 5. For a consultation of the entry for Stoke Canon (Devon), Exeter, Dean and Chapter, ms. 3672, pp. 100-1 (mid 14th-century cartulary of Exeter cathedral).

10. H.C.Maxwell Lyte, 'Domesday Book', Pall Mall Magazine, 37 (May-August 1902), 209-16.

11. For the publication of Domesday Book, M.M.Condon and E.M.Hallam, 'Government printing of the Public Records in the eighteenth century', Journal of the Society of Archivists, 7 (1984), 373-83.

12. There are at present no VCH Domesday translations for Cheshire, Gloucestershire and Lincolnshire. The first of these will appear shortly.

13. S.Denne, 'Doubts and conjectures concerning the reason commonly assigned for inserting or omitting the words ecclesia and presbyter in Domesday Book', Archaeologia, 8 (1787), 218-38.

14. Exeter Cathedral Library, ms. X.52. On Lyttleton, see R.W.Finn, Domesday Studies: the Liber Exoniensis (London, 1964), 4.

15. R.W.Eyton, 'Notes on Domesday', Transactions of the Shropshire Archaeological Society, 1 (1878), 100. It should be pointed out that this view was based solely on the Inquisitio Gheldi in Exon, which Eyton believed to date from 1084.

16. The Phillimore editions provide the most recent guide to place-name identifications as well as making some new identifications. See especially the volumes for Devon, Herefordshire, Somerset, Warwickshire and Wiltshire. See also Bates, A Bibliography, for the most recent identifications, notably nos. 1124, 1791, 2142, 4223.

17. D.Crouch, The Beaumont twins: the roots and branches of power in the twelfth century (Cambridge, 1986), 117.

18. J.H.Round, 'Domesday Book', in Feudal England (2nd edn, London, 1961), 17-34, 106-120.

19. Maitland, 3.

20. E.A.Freeman, The History of the Norman Conquest of England, its causes and its results, 6 vols. (Oxford, 1867-79), 5, 3-11.

21. Galbraith's theories were first published in 1942, V.H.Galbraith, 'The making of Domesday Book', EHR, 57 (1942), 161-77, and developed finally in The Making of Domesday Book (Oxford, 1961).

22. C.Johnson, 'Domesday Survey', in VCH Norfolk, 2 (London, 1906), 1-4. For Douglas's general views, D.C.Douglas, 'The Domesday

Survey', History, 21 (1937), 249-57.   There is an appreciation of Douglas's Domesday Book work by R.H.C.Davis, 'David Charles Douglas 1898-1982', Proceedings of the British Academy, 69 (1983), 516-18.

23.   V.H.Galbraith,   Domesday Book: its place in administrative history (Oxford, 1974), 14.

24.   S.P.J.Harvey, 'Domesday Book and its predecessors', EHR, 86 (1971), 753-73.   See also, F.F.Kreisler, 'Domesday Book and the Anglo-Norman synthesis', in W.C.Jordan et al (eds.), Order and Innovation in the Middle Ages: Essays in honor of Joseph R. Strayer (Princeton, 1976), 3-16, for similar arguments.

25.   D.R.Roffe, 'The Lincolnshire hundred', Landscape History, 3 (1981), 32-3.

26.   For the various hidage lists in the Domesday Monachorum, Harvey, 'Domesday Book and its predessors', 756-9.

27.   S.P.J.Harvey, 'Domesday Book and Anglo-Norman Governance', TRHS, 5th. series, 5 (1975), 183-90.   For other comments on the role of the hundred, H.B.Clarke, 'The Domesday Satellites', in Sawyer, DB, a reassessment, 57-62.

28.   S.P.J.Harvey, 'Taxation and the Ploughland in Domesday Book', in Sawyer, DB, a reassessment, 86-103.

29.   L.Musset, 'Les domaines de l'époque franque et les destinées du régime domanial du IXe au XIe siècle', Bulletin de la société des antiquaires de Normandie, 49 (1946, for 1942-5), 65-6.

30.   Maitland, 460-1; J.A.Green, 'The last century of Danegeld', EHR, 96 (1981), 243.

31.   Anglo-Saxon Chronicle, 'E', 1090, 1096, 1098, 1100.

32.   W.Stubbs, Select Charters, and other illustrations of English Constitutional History from the earliest times to the reign of Edward the First, 9th edn (Oxford, 1913), 119, clauses 11, 13.   But note that Danegeld was apparently being taken on manorial demesne in 1129-30, Green, 'Last century of Danegeld', 246.

33.   C. and F.Thorn, Domesday Book. 9. Devon, 2 vols. (Chichester, 1985), 2, 'Exon. Extra Information and Discrepancies with DB'.

34.   C. and F.Thorn, Domesday Book. 16. Worcestershire (Chichester, 1982), Appendix V, discussing and translating the document described as 'Worcester B', with references to other literature.

35.   V.H.Galbraith and J.Tait (eds.), Herefordshire Domesday, circa 1160-1170, Pipe Roll Society, 63 (new series, 25) (London, 1950).

36. Hallam, Domesday through nine centuries, 73.

37. Hallam, 175.

38. Curia Regis Rolls of the Reigns of Richard I and John, 3, 333. On ancient demesne, see the interesting remarks of P.R.Hyams, Kings, Lords and Peasants in Medieval England (Oxford, 1980), 246-9.

39. See in general, S.F.C.Milsom, The Legal Framework of English Feudalism (Cambridge, 1976).

40. For Agarde's published work, see appendices to R.Gale, Registrum Honoris de Richmond, exhibens terrarum et villarum quae quondam fuerunt Edwini comitis infra Richmondshire descriptionem, ex Libro Domesday (London, 1722). For an appreciation, Hallam, Domesday Book through nine centuries, 115-17.

41. On Robert Brady, see D.C.Douglas, English Scholars (London, 1939), 170-3; Hallam, Domesday Book through nine centuries, 124-7.

42. M.Hale, The Primitive Organisation of Mankind, considered and explained according to the Light of Nature (London, 1677), 236-7.

43. Hallam, Domesday Book through nine centuries, 62.

44. J.H.Round, 'Notes on Domesday measures of land', in P.E.Dove (ed.), Domesday Studies: being the papers read at the meetings of the Domesday Commemoration 1886, 2 vols. (London, 1888-91), 1, 189-225; 'Domesday Book', in Feudal England, 98-100; VCH, Somerset, 1, 388-93.

45. J.H.Round, 'Domesday Book', in Feudal England, 1, 47-76, especially at 51.

46. For Round and the VCH, W.R.Powell, 'J.Horace Round, the County Historian: the Victoria County Histories and the Essex Archaeological Society', Transactions of the Essex Archaeological Society, 3rd. series, 12 (1981), 25-38.

47. J.Tait, in EHR, 12 (1897), 768-77.

48. See, for example, J.Tait, 'Large Hides and Small Hides', EHR, 17 (1902), 280-2; H.M.Cam, 'The Evolution of the Medieval English Franchise', Speculum, 32 (1957), 427-42 (reprinted in Law-finders and Law-makers in Medieval England (London, 1962), 22-43); T.H.Aston, 'The Origins of the Manor in England', TRHS, 5th. series, 8 (1958), 59-83 (reprinted with 'a postscript' in T.H.Aston et al [eds.], Social Relations and Ideas: Essays in Honour of R.H.Hilton [Cambridge, 1983], 1-43).

49. See, for example, R.Abels, 'Bookland and Fyrd Service in Late Saxon England', in R.A.Brown (ed.), Anglo-Norman Studies, VII, Proceedings of the Battle Conference 1984 (Woodbridge, 1985), 16-25.

50. Maitland, 520.

51. H.C.Darby, Domesday England (Cambridge, 1977), 384.

52. H.C.Darby, 'Domesday Woodland in East Anglia', Antiquity, 8 (1934), 211-15.

53. Darby, Domesday England, 375-84.

54. Darby, 383.

55. W.J.Ford, 'Some Settlement Patterns in the Central Region of the Warwickshire Avon', in P.H.Sawyer (ed.), Medieval Settlement: Continuity and Change (London, 1976), 274-94 (reprinted in P.H.Sawyer [ed.], English Medieval Settlement [London, 1979], 143-63).

56. Darby, Domesday England, 13.

57. W.G.Hoskins, 'The Highland Zone in Domesday Book', in Provincial England: Essays in Social and Economic History (London, 1964), 15-52.

58. For a general treatment of this problem, C.C.Taylor, Village and Farmstead: a History of Rural Settlement in England (London, 1983), chapters 8 and 10.

59. R.J.Ivens, 'Deddington Castle, Oxfordshire, and the English Honour of Odo of Bayeux', Oxoniensia, 49 (1985), 101-19.

60. The pioneer study was J.Campbell, 'Observations on English Government from the Tenth to the Twelfth Century', TRHS, 5th. series, 25 (1975), 39-54. See further, J.Percival, 'The Precursors of Domesday: Roman and Carolingian Land Registers', in Sawyer, DB, a Reassessment, 5-27.

61. A.L. Léchaudé d'Anisy and H.-J., J.-R., Sainte-Marie, Recherches sur le Domesday ou Liber censualis d'Angleterre (Caen, 1842).

62. O.Rackham, Ancient Woodland: Its History, Vegetation and Uses in England (London, 1980), chapter 9; S.P.J.Harvey, 'The Extent and Profitability of Demesne Agriculture in England in the Later Eleventh Century', in T.H.Aston, Social Relations, 45-72.

63. <u>Domesday Rebound</u> (2nd edn, London, 1965), is extremely important.

64. The same point is made by S.P.J.Harvey, 'Recent Domesday Studies',
    <u>EHR</u>, 95 (1980), 133, and by Clarke, in Sawyer, <u>DB, a Reassessment</u>,
    68. There are some maps of landholding in 1066 in D.Hill, <u>An Atlas</u>
    <u>of Anglo-Saxon England</u> (Oxford, 1981), 101-6.

THE MAKING OF DOMESDAY BOOK

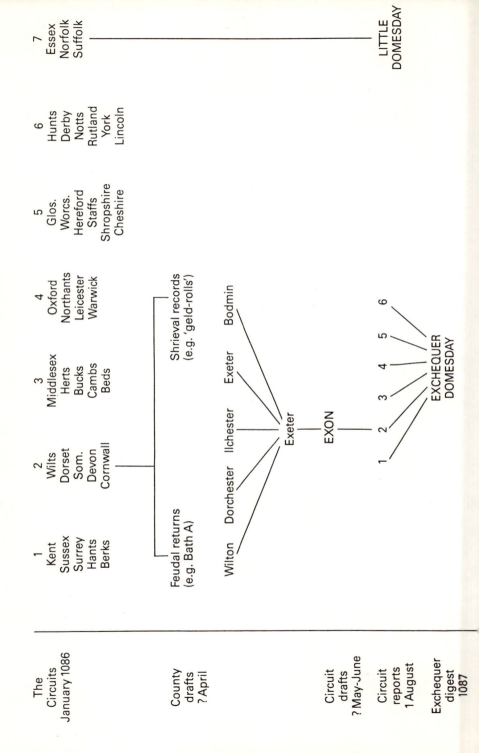

Domesday Book : an Introduction

FRANK BARLOW

William the Conqueror, at his Christmas court at Gloucester in 1085, ordered that a descriptio, a survey, of his kingdom should be made. It was probably also decided at the same time that the annual land-tax, Danegeld or geld, should be collected at the high rate of 6s. the hide. While these operations were being carried out he remained in England, but felt free to return to Normandy in the late summer of the following year. Twelve months later, he invaded the French Vexin and, as the result of an injury, died at Rouen on 9 September 1087. In England he was succeeded by his second son, William Rufus.(1)

No one tells us exactly why William ordered this 'Domesday' survey to be made. Most of those who mention it thought it rather bizarre. I think that few men knew. Kings did not have to explain their actions; their word was law; and the Conqueror was notoriously taciturn and inscrutable. In this introductory lecture I will leave the consideration of causes and objectives to the end, for they can be inferred only from the procedures employed and the contents of the several reports produced by the surveyors. I will try first to explain, as simply as possible, how the survey may have been made, identify the most important surviving reports and give some idea of their contents.

The modus operandi has been studied intensively in the last hundred years by a series of most distinguished scholars, notably F. W. Maitland, J. H. Round, V. H. Galbraith, one of my own teachers, and R. Welldon Finn. Although a scenario, complete and firm in every detail, is unlikely ever to be produced, there is now a fair amount of agreement among historians on the main steps and features. And this consensus hinges on an interpretation of the Exon, or Exeter, Domesday, a manuscript normally kept in the Dean and Chapter library at Exeter - the view that it was a preliminary regional draft of the survey. This theory, apparently first propounded by Lord Lyttleton in 1756 and, more publicly, by F. H. Baring in 1912, was, however, 'rubbished' by Round, since it was incompatible with his own ideas; and it was not until the 1940s and 50s that Galbraith reaffirmed Baring's interpretation and developed and popularized a general thesis which, although it has been subsequently modified here and there in detail, seems to be unchallengeable in outline. Naturally I will give as much attention to Exon as I can.(2)

William discussed the proposed survey with his counsellors over the Christmas festival. It is likely that he wanted quick results, partly because he was an impatient sort of man, partly because he knew he would have to be at hand while the survey was being carried out. He never cared to spend too long in England. As far as we can see, there were no exact precedents for what he set on foot.(3) But all his counsellors, bishops, earls and barons, were, like him, great landowners who had been involved in the enormous change of ownership which had followed the Conquest. They were practical and experienced men of affairs, each with his own team of land agents.(4)

The administrative machinery which allowed this vast project to be carried out so quickly, and apparently so smoothly, was already in existence. And a duality should be noticed which can be seen throughout the operation of its products. On the one hand there were the feudal estates, the honours, of the tenants-in-chief that I have just mentioned. These, like the royal estates, the royal demesne, were scattered more or less across the kingdom. Thus the kingdom was composed of a mosaic of feudal honours. But, on the other hand, this, often fluctuating, pattern was laid across the more ancient and permanent territorial administrative units of the kingdom, the shires or counties, which in turn were divided into the hundreds and wapentakes. In each shire was a royal sheriff with a royal castle, and sometimes there was a bishop. Each shire and hundred or wapentake had a court. Also the king had the power to send out commissioners or judges on circuit in order to control or supplement the activities of his local officers. At Christmas 1085, therefore, the king could have organized the survey either on strictly feudal lines - ordering each holder of lands to make a return - or entrust it essentially to his own servants.

He chose the latter course, deciding to use the machinery of royal government. England was divided into probably seven groups of shires, each containing 3 to 6 according to size, and a team of royal legati or commissioners was appointed to each circuit, as these units are usually called. Circuit no. 2 (using Carl Stephenson's numeration) consisted of the 5 shires of Wiltshire, Dorset, Somerset, Devon and Cornwall. The commissioners were probably small parties of prelates and barons, assisted by one or more clerks and perhaps monks. We are fortunate in knowing from the tax records in Exon that in Circuit 2 Bishop William and his colleagues were succeeded by Walter and his colleagues.(5) We may confidently identify the former with William of St Calais, bishop of Durham. Walter, however, could be anyone. If, however, we look for barons with Westcountry connections - and we may be looking in completely the wrong direction - possibilities are Walter Giffard, a cousin of the king who later became earl of Buckingham (although he was one of the commissioners on Circuit 5),(6) Walter de Douai, lord of Bampton in Devon and Castle Carey in Somerset, or Walter Hosat, soon to be sheriff of Wiltshire. However that may be, the commissioners, whether strangers to the district or local landowners, made use of the sheriffs and the county and hundredal organizations and also of the local tenants-in-chief or their agents. Hence, at almost every stage of the survey, there was a choice between a feudal or territorial presentation of the findings. And the final pattern may not have been decided until towards the end of the exercise.

There were other basic discordances. We must remember that there were Frenchmen and Englishmen involved, each giving evidence in his own language, and that the language of government was Latin. Thus oral reports would have been made in dialects of English and French, but written reports in English or Latin (I doubt whether there was much written French). And all the official reports were in Latin. The Domesday terminology is, therefore, divorced from social and agricultural realities and has to be interpreted. I need hardly remind you that all records were written by hand on parchment, in shorthand, and that scribes varied in ability. There has been a tendency among historians to refer to rolls, e.g. the geld rolls, perhaps because later the basic records of the Exchequer were Pipe Rolls. But, as far as Domesday Book is concerned, evidence is strong that in general, from the beginning to the end, sheets of parchment folded into two (bifolia), and, if necessary, organized into larger quires, were the ordinary materials.

Among the first things that the king and his advisers had to decide were the terms of the inquiry, although we must hold in mind that these could have been modified – and probably were – as the operation proceeded. No official schedule has survived; but a list preserved at Ely Abbey of questions that the commissioners had to put to the local authorities and communities, and which had to be answered on oath, agrees for the most part with the information collected, and can be given some credence.(7) We can see from the schedule and the reports that it had been decided that the micro-unit of the survey should be the manor and not the township or vill. The manor was the normal administrative and economic unit in all the feudal honours and also a unit responsible for the payment of the land tax, geld. Thus it, too, had its duality. Geographically, in some areas it corresponded more or less to a village; in others there was little correspondence.

The questions to be answered in respect of each manor were, according to the Ely list: (1) What is its name? (2) Who held it in the time of King Edward? and (3) Who holds it now? (4) How many hides does it contain? (this means: what is its rating to the geld?) (5) How many ploughs are there on the demesne (home farm)? and (6) How many among the villeins (the tenant farmers)? (7) How many villeins, cottagers and slaves, freemen and sokemen are there? (8) How much woodland? (9) How much meadowland? (10) How many mills? (11) How much has been added or taken away ? (12) How much was the whole manor worth, and how much now? (13) How much did each freeman and sokeman have, and how much now? (14) Could more (profit) be had from it than is now obtained? No doubt by mistake, the Ely schedule omits the inquiry into the demesne live-stock, which was undoubtedly one of the original features of the survey.

Let us now turn to the actual conduct of the survey. There is no good reason to think that William at this stage set up an operations HQ at Winchester, the seat of the royal treasury. He was, however, there at Easter, as was his custom when in England, and he spent Whitsun at Westminster. As he travelled around, all the queries, complaints etc would have been addressed to him in his itinerant court and answered by him or his counsellors. The stream of correspondence must have swollen considerably; but, remarkably, little of it has survived.(8) It is a period badly illustrated by royal writs, and the king's movements cannot be traced.

There are, however, two royal charters with good witness lists that can be dated to 1086.(9) The one with the longer list records a royal court held on a Sunday at Lacock in Wiltshire, a manor on the fief of William of Eu, the son of the count, who was in attendance on his royal lord. The Conqueror was accompanied by the two sons who were to succeed him in turn in England, William Rufus and Henry, by both archbishops, seven of the most important English bishops and his great servant, Geoffrey bishop of Coutances; by three counts or earls, his half-brother Robert of Mortain, the Breton Alan Rufus and Roger of Montgomery; by more than a dozen major barons; by two abbots, Serlo of Gloucester and the infamous Thurstin of Glastonbury; and by several important household officials, including Eudo dapifer and Robert dispensator. Notable absentees were the king's other half-brother, Odo of Bayeux, who was in prison, and his eldest son, Robert, who was in self-imposed exile. But this was a most imposing gathering of the king's family in its closest and its widest aspects. While the survey was being carried out, William was operating with his greatest vassals. We should note that, although there were at least one Italian and Lotharingian and two Bretons in his recorded company, there were no Englishmen. The aged Wulfstan bishop of Worcester, whom we may have expected to get as far as Gloucester, had not ventured to travel to Wiltshire. I expect, however, that some of William's clerks and certainly his huntsmen would have been natives.

 It would have been a company such as this which had assembled for the Christmas court at Gloucester in 1085. The survey could have been initiated in one of two ways. Either writs were sent to every sheriff giving instructions for the operation to start. Or, and perhaps more likely, the commissioners were appointed and went off to their regions. Of the five legati we know by name all but one were present at Lacock, and the brother of the absentee was there.(10) The commissioners when appointed would probably have visited each county court in turn (in the case of Circuit 2, Wilton, Dorchester, Ilchester, Exeter and Bodmin) and given the necessary instructions to the sheriffs and suitors. And, in this circuit, they may well have decided to make Exeter their own HQ and recruited a staff of scribes from the several monasteries and cathedral churches in the region. Almost all the preliminary work must have been left to the sheriffs, who were required to produce a report for their county, and, presumably send it in to the provincial HQ by a certain date. Easter Day, which fell on 5 April in 1086, might be considered too early; Whitsunday, 24 May, would seem just about right. But my guess would be Lady day (25 March) or Easter. Both were important financial terms and deadlines are always unreasonable.

The sheriffs, when instructed, would in turn have given orders to the suitors of the shire court and the hundred courts and got the inquiry into motion. Already in existence were some useful records concerned with the ordinary processes of royal and manorial administration. The sheriffs had the so-called 'geld-rolls', lists of estates with their hidage, their assessment to geld, arranged under hundreds. They also knew all about the royal demesne and the cities and boroughs, for they were in charge of them. Seigneurial land agents, bailiffs and reeves had more or less elaborate records of the estates under their care. Church estates probably had the best. It is likely that the sheriff provided for each hundred a skeleton return, listing each manor, which had to be checked for accuracy and amplified with the required detail. At the same time the tenants-in-chief holding in the shire would be required to list their manors, assign them a value and provide such other relevant information as they had. A survey of seven demesne manors held by Bath Abbey, known as Bath A, represents the information provided by that tenant-in-chief in 1086.(11)

It is likely that all those involved in the inquiry presented their findings on oath. Juries representing each township, consisting of the priest, reeve and six good men, probably swore in the hundred courts. In the shire courts it was the turn of the sheriff, the barons and their French vassals and the hundredal juries - the last composed of four foreigners and four natives. The final result of this phase of the operation should have been a series of answers in respect of every manor in the county, grouped under separate hundreds and, in fact, in the order which they were to keep until the end.

These county reports, none of which has survived, are considered to have been the most idiosyncratic and at the same time the least rectifiable ingredients in the whole process. Factual corrections could be made only with difficulty after this point. The many lacunae in the regional and final reports make this clear. It was the task of the HQ staff to turn this rather intractable material into a regional survey. For Circuit 2, about a dozen clerks, assembled presumably at Exeter cathedral, produced _Exon_. The bishop was Osbern fitzOsbern, a Norman, once Edward the Confessor's clerk. The clerks were obviously recruited from various monasteries and churches. One seems to have come from St Peter's Bath; another wrote many books for the new cathedral at Salisbury. The hand of the royal clerk who penned the final version of the survey, probably at Winchester, can be recognized on at least one page. Most were involved at the same time and place, passing the bifolia from hand to hand. All wrote what is known as Carolingian minuscule, some better than others. On the whole the calligraphy of _Exon_ is not impressive. The scribes were working at speed, under pressure, and _Exon_ has all the characteristics of a hasty draft. Most modern commentators have noticed its disorderly appearance, reflecting muddle only partially corrected.(12) The local director, whoever he may

have been, made one change in the organization of the material which is
unique. The several feudal honours were assembled, although still in
identifiable county order, on the circuit basis. For example, the fief
of the count of Mortain extends over the counties of Devon, Cornwall and
Somerset, that of Tavistock Abbey over Dorset, Devon and Cornwall.
Also, as with the other regional surveys, lists of disputes over land
and usurpations, in Exon called Terrae occupatae, were prepared. These
occur at the end of Exon proper. Finally, some summaries of the lands
of a few fiefs (perhaps originally of all) were made.

Although we are accustomed to think of Exon, together with the more
advanced stages of the report, as books, it must be recognized that this
is only their modern form. All consisted originally of a number of
self-contained booklets, each devoted to a single classified group of
manors. And these, of course, could be arranged and re-arranged at
will. Exon consisted, and consists, of a series of booklets each
devoted to an individual honour and running across the shire divisions.
It was first bound up, and in an arbitrary order, at the end of the
fourteenth century, and by that time almost the whole of Wiltshire, the
greater part of Dorset and some of Devon had been lost. There were also
gaps in the associated material.

While the regional surveys were being drafted it seems that a
second set of royal commissioners - in this case, we are told, with no
local connections - was sent round to deal with problems which had
arisen, and particularly to settle as many as possible of the disputes
over title which had emerged. As a geld at 6s. the hide was also in
process of collection, perhaps these legati were engaged in supervising
this. Significantly, bound up with Exon are summary geld accounts for
Wiltshire, Dorset, Cornwall and (in part) Somerset.

One bit of correspondence which might have come from this stage has
survived from Circuit 7, East Anglia and Essex. Archbishop Lanfranc
of Canterbury replied to a correspondent, whose name is reduced to S.,
that he had no land in demesne in Essex: it was all in the hands of his
monks. When I published this letter I suggested that S. was Swegn,
sheriff of Essex. Galbraith later imagined him to be Samson, a clerk to
whom he attributed a large part of the organization. I still prefer my
own suggestion.(13)

The next process at the regional HQs was to make a fair copy of
their report and send it off to the king. For Circuit 2 we have only
the rough draft. For Circuit 7, East Anglia and Essex, we have only the
fair copy. It is the document known as Little Domesday. And, although
it resembles Exon in general appearance, its organization is different:
the several feudal honours are divided up between the three component
shires. And it is possible, though unlikely, that the fair copy of Exon
was also on this model. It is widely thought that it was these
provincial surveys which were delivered to the king in August when he
was in Wiltshire making his last arrangements before going abroad. On 1
August at Old Salisbury he took oaths of fealty from all the major
barons and their honorial vassals, that is to say, all important holders

of land. And there may have been some connection between that event and the Domesday survey.

Nineteen months had passed since the survey had been inaugurated. And it would seem that it was in the following twelve months, which ended with the Conqueror's death, that the final version, generally known as the Exchequer Domesday, was made. The king and his counsellors and probably the treasury clerks who were supposed to make use of its findings, were obviously of the opinion that the results in the form of the regional surveys were unmanageable. It was therefore decided to produce a digest. This Exchequer Domesday, although a misfortune for historians, is a very remarkable editorial achievment. The regional surveys were reduced to a series of county booklets, each written neatly in double column. The formulae were shortened and standardized, the words abbreviated drastically and all information considered superfluous was jettisoned. Among the most serious losses are the statistics about farm animals and most surnames of tenants; and detail is often shed through consolidation. If there had been a plan to produce totals of various kinds, this too was abandoned. It is now believed by those most expert in the subject that it is the work of a single editor and scribe. Galbraith wanted to make him Samson, a Norman royal clerk whom Rufus made bishop of Worcester.(14) But there is internal evidence, especially from the revision of the spelling of placenames, that the scribe was either an Englishman or had lived in the kingdom for a long time.

Whoever he may have been, he did not finish his task. The Circuit 7 report, for East Anglia and Essex, was left unedited. It was tarted up a bit with rubrics to make it look a little more like the rest and given a colophon: 'In the year of the Lord 1086, which is the twentieth of William's reign, this _descriptio_ was made, not only through these three shires but also through the rest.' Why this 'Little Domesday' was left unedited remains a matter of controversy. Some scholars believe that its complexity made its reduction beyond the powers of the Winchester editor. This I do not believe. It would just have needed more and harder work. It is simpler to think that the king's death brought the operation virtually to an end. Fortunately for historians. If only we had _Exon_ or Little Domesday for the whole of England!

Why then was the survey set on foot at Christmas 1085 and pushed through? Let us look briefly at the historical background. In the course of 1085 William learnt that Cnut II of Denmark had formed a naval coalition and was preparing once more to invade England and assert his claim to the throne. William crossed to England with a large mercenary army he had recruited and billeted it on the various baronial courts. Cnut was murdered in July 1086 before he could set sail. And in August William returned to the Continent. It is natural to think that the immediate cause of the survey was the invasion scare. True, William did not inquire very pointedly into the military resources of the kingdom. In some of the returns the territorial duty of army and navy service is occasionally mentioned, and this, like the geld, was linked with the hidage.(15) But there was no investigation of knight service or castle-guard. Castles are rarely identified and there are no returns of knights.

The late Victorians thought that Domesday Book was a geld-book - a record of liability to the land tax. And, despite the great reaction against that view, so obviously it was. Every effort was made to record the hidage and to discover hides that had never paid geld or had been lost to the record. We must never forget that a heavy geld was being collected to pay for the king's war expenses, including the wages of his mercenaries, while the survey was being conducted. But the inquiry was into more than the hidage. Two other questions seem basic - who owns and who owned the manor? and what is and was it worth? That is what the Anglo-Saxon Chronicler particularly noted when he wrote the Conqueror's obituary: 'By his guile England was so scrutinized that there was not a single hide of which he did not discover the owner and how much it was worth, and then set it down in writing.' Domesday Book is, for the higher echelons of society, a comprehensive land register and also a rent-book or rental. And it may be thought that the manorial details which were originally required in such detail, although in the end partly discarded, were in connection with the valuations. As we know from Anglo-Saxon wills, live-stock and men went in the same breath as land. And the maintenance of both at the optimum level was a prime duty of any land agent. The Domesday figures for animals, we should notice, are for the lord's demesne. If villeins had animals, besides their plough beasts, they go unrecorded because they did not contribute to the value of the manor.

How was it then that the statistics of the demesne live-stock were discarded? It may have been realized that the animal population was subject to wide fluctuations, and with 1086 such a bad year for farmers the figures were inconveniently low. Or, when it was decided to compress, someone simply rated this the least valuable information. The directors of the operation were, as usual, southerners and lowlanders. They were interested in ploughs, not sheep. But we should not assume that the provincial surveys were destroyed when the digest was made. The animal statistics were surely available for some years to anyone interested in this feature.

As a land register, which led immediately to the recording and settlement of many disputes over ownership, the survey was of value to every holder of land. As a rental, it was specially valuable to the king. It may be that he had had disputes with the barons in the last months of 1085 about their contributions to the defence of the kingdom against the threatened invasion and over what they could afford. The billeting of the mercenaries on them could have led to much trouble. And a record of the value of the several honours would be of long-standing use to the king in the exploitation of his various rights of lordship in them. One has only to think of aids, wardships, reliefs and the sale of heirs.

Victorians also thought that the Domesday survey was in preparation for a reform of the tax system. The reaction against this 'anachronistic idea' has, I think, gone much too far in recent years. The Conqueror was not, of course, a fiscal reformer in the Victorian mould, solicitous for the interest of his subjects, especially the lower orders. It was notorious that his actions were inspired by avarice and self-interest. But this should encourage us to think that he was indeed wondering whether lucrative changes in the taxation system might not be possible. Strong kings did in fact introduce changes to their advantage whenever possible. The information produced by the Domesday survey could have been exploited in several ways. The manors or the honours could have been re-rated to the geld, or a new tax could have been levied on ploughs and ploughlands.(16) The last expedient was actually tried out in the twelfth century.

Why then, as with disputes over land, did not fiscal changes immediately follow the survey? Surely because its originator died. What the powerful Conqueror could have forced through was completely beyond the capability of his initially weak successor. And by the time that Rufus had consolidated his authority he was doing nicely by exploiting the existing system to the full.

Finally, just a few words about the reliability and the exploitability of the record. Evaluation of the Domesday survey and its reports has fluctuated. Until fairly recently it was regarded as a stupendous achievement and its statistics a miracle of accuracy. More detailed work and a collation of the several drafts and such associated records as exist – particularly taxation schedules – have shown that at every stage there was an accumulation of every possible type of error. And, one may ask, how could it possibly be otherwise? Everyone knows that statistics are either lies or damned lies. And it is ironical that it is at the very time when the fallibility of the record is being generally accepted that the statistics are being put on computers so that more accurate totals and analyses than ever before can be obtained. However, I would not simply say, 'Garbage in, garbage out'. Although Domesday figures should be used with care, they are very much better than nothing. In 1086 a large number of very hard-working and hard-pressed men tried to answer questions put to them and the result is not a gigantic fraud, rather a flawed masterpiece. We should by all means look a gift horse in the mouth, but in order to see its strengths and weaknesses and so be enabled to get the greatest possible profit out of it.

Yet, despite the immense amount of work on the elucidation of Domesday Book, it remains a difficult source to understand and use. Earlier in this lecture I listed the Ely schedule of questions to which answers had to be found. Let us, in conclusion, look at the answers which were actually given in respect of one manor. And I take as example the manor of Kenton on the estuary of the Exe.(17) We are told in Exon, roughly in the order of the Ely questionnaire, that the king holds Kenton and Queen Edith (i.e. King Edward's wife) held it in 1066; and it pays geld for 3 hides and 1 ferling (i.e. one-sixteenth of a hide: the fraction is an inter-linear addition). These hides, it says, could be ploughed by 20 ploughs. It continues: the manor is divided between the king, who has in demesne (i.e., on the home farm) 1 hide and 4 ploughs, and the villeins (i.e., tenant farmers), who have 2 hides and 1 ferling and 15 ploughs. We have now reached question 7, and are informed that the king has there 30 villeins, 10 bordars (i.e., cottagers), 6 slaves, 4 swineherds, who pay 20s. p.a., 8 salt-makers, who also pay 20s. p.a., 20 animals (presumably draught beasts), 200 sheep and 20 goats, 1 mill, which pays 50d., woodland 1/2 a league long and 4 furlongs wide, 10 acres of meadow and 150 acres of pasture. The manor is worth £30 a year.

Such a return, which is typical, cannot be understood either topographically or economically from the statistics given. It has to be interpreted with reference, on the one hand, to our general understanding of eleventh-century social and economic conditions and, on the other, to the actual landscape and local knowledge. From the former we can assume that Kenton consisted of a home farm surrounded by a number of subordinate tenant farmers. From the latter, some locations can be suggested. The head (<u>caput</u>) of the manor was presumably Court Hall, which is adjacent to the parish church, and the seigneurial demesne may be represented by neighbouring Ford Farm. The animals are presumably the stock of that home farm and the 6 slaves would have been responsible for, among other things, the 4 ploughs in use. W. G. Hoskins postulated that the number of <u>villani</u> give, in Devon, the number of tenant farmers, each with a separate homestead.(18) But 30 seems rather a lot, and we notice that they had only 15 ploughs between them. Anyhow, we may be sure that most of their homesteads are represented by the many farms still existing in the area. We can also guess that the cottagers lived mostly in the village of Kenton and that some of them were tradesmen. The mill and the salt-pans can be located in the Powderham area.

We can thus build up a picture of the manor in rough outline, with the greater the local knowledge, the greater the detail. And in doing so we become aware of the absence of some information which is occasionally given elsewhere and of other facts which were either considered irrelevant or taken for granted. Presumably the twentieth plough was missing from the home farm. But why no mention of the church or dependent chapels and of the clergy who served them? Were there no female slaves or bee-keepers? No horses or cows? How many swine had the swineherds? What services, labour and others, did the villeins and cottagers owe to the home farm? What does the additional one-sixteenth of a hide signify? Surely something that has once been added, perhaps a homestead? But two and one-sixteenth hides among 30 (or 15) farms just doesn't go. The only divisors are 3 and 11. Was the ferling the assessment on the cottagers? Somewhere there is an irregularity or mistake.

Whenever we get down to the nitty-gritty we are apt to run into often insoluble problems of interpretation. But we should not be surprised or complain. We should be thankful for what we are given and regard the puzzles as a bonus. The Domesday Survey is worthy of all the protracted and intensive study it has been given. It is a pool of information that is unlikely ever to be completely exhausted. And it can be trawled for many different kinds of fish.

Notes

1. For a comprehensive bibliography, see David Bates, Bibliography of Domesday Book (Woodbridge,1986).

2. For Exon, see particularly V.H.Galbraith, 'The Making of Domesday Book', EHR, lvii (1942); R.Welldon Finn, Domesday Studies: the Liber Exoniensis (London, 1964); H.B.Clarke, 'The Domesday Satellites', Domesday Book: a reassessment [henceforth, DB, reassessment], ed. Peter Sawyer (London, 1985), pp.50-70; Alexander R. Rumble, 'The Palaeography of the Domesday Manuscripts', ibid., pp.28-49.

3. Cf. John Percival, 'The precursors of Domesday: Roman and Carolingian Land Registers', DB, reassessment, pp.5-27; Sally P.J. Harvey, 'Taxation and the ploughland In Domesday Book', ibid., pp. 101-2.

4. It is tempting to think that Ranulf Flambard, who became a great financial officer and royal factotum in the next reign, was involved in the planning. Cf. Galbraith, Domesday Book, its Place in Administrative History [henceforth, DB, Place], (Oxford, 1974), pp. 104-5; Sally P.J.Harvey, 'Domesday Book and Anglo-Norman Governance', TRHS, 5th ser., xxv (1975), 190-2, 'Taxation and the ploughland', DB, reassessment, pp.100-1. But he seems to have been in the itinerant royal court in 1086-7 and could not have been engaged in the final stages: see F.Barlow, William Rufus (London, 1983), pp. 195, 199, 243-6.

5. DB, iii. 2-3.

6. See below, n.10. If Walter Giffard was in the first set for circuit 5, he could well have been in the second set for circuit 2.

7. For Inquisitio Eliensis and the editions, see Clarke, 'The Domesday Satellites', p. 53.

8. Correspondence concerning a dispute between the bishop of Worcester and the abbot of Evesham is in Regesta, i, nos. 184, 221, 230 (in 221 Adam [de Port] should be corrected to Adam brother of Eudo dapifer). See also below, nn. 10, 13.

9. Regesta, nos. 220 (cf. DB, i. 71b), 232. It is possible that the former (at Lacock) can be associated with the king's important visit to Wiltshire in August: see below, p. 20.

10. William bishop of Durham (circuit 2); Remigius bishop of Lincoln, earl Walter Giffard, Henry de Ferrers and Adam brother of Eudo dapifer (circuit 5): Hemingi Chartularium, ed. T.Hearne (Oxford, 1723), i, 288.

11. Clarke, 'The Domesday Satellites', pp. 60, 64.

12. Finn, Liber Exoniensis, pp. 147 ff.; Rumble, as in note 2.

13. F.Barlow, 'Domesday Book: a letter of Lanfranc', EHR, lxxviii (1963), 284-9, reprinted, with an additional note, in The Norman Conquest and Beyond (London, 1983).

14. Galbraith, 'Notes on the career of Samson, bishop of Worcester (1096-1112)', EHR, lxxii (1967), 86, DB, place, pp. 50-1, 69-70, 105.

15. For hidage and military service, especially in circuit 3, see Richard Abels, 'Bookland and Fyrd Service in Late Saxon England', Anglo-Norman Studies VII, ed. R.Allen Brown (Woodbridge, 1985), 1-25.

16. Harvey, 'Domesday Book and Anglo-Norman Governance', pp. 186 ff., 'Taxation and the ploughland'. Cf. Barlow, William Rufus, pp. 199 and n., 243-7.

17. DB, iii. 94b; i. 100b.

18. W.G.Hoskins, 'The Highland Zone in Domesday Book', Provincial England (London, 1965), 15-52 especially pp. 33, 43 ff.

The Geography of Exeter Domesday: Cornwall and Devon

WILLIAM RAVENHILL

Geographers seem to come and go in generations; of the two most recent, the earlier was distinctly landscape oriented, the members of the present one, it is claimed, should be literate, numerate and graphicate. There is much to be said for bridging this generation gap, to look at the Domesday record bifocally.(1) In so doing one cannot but be struck at the very outset how in so many respects the association of the two words Domesday and Geography amounts to a contradiction in terms. Domesday Book demonstrably belongs to the class of written documents and is to the fore among them in importance; it abounds with numeracy but it is decidedly, and much to be regretted, non-graphicate.

Domesday Book belongs to that period in our history when the inspired, theoretical cartography of the Greeks and the practical cartography of the Romans had long since been forgotten in North-West Europe. The movement of the Normans, a dynamic war-like people, into Normandy and subsequently into England can be contrasted with their conquest of Southern Italy, and especially Sicily. In that conquest they came into contact with the classical cartographic tradition which had been kept alive by the Muslims whose scholars, imbued with Ptolemaic Geography, saw to its improvement, application and diffusion with the expansion of the Islamic Empire. That the seeds of Geography fell on fertile ground in Sicily under the Normans is not in doubt, seeds subsequently to flower in the build-up of knowledge about the world which, by inculcating a global outlook, was to change markedly the history of Europe.

No such legacy survived in Britain to pass on to the Normans; it was a land and a culture without maps and, most surprisingly for a military people, the Normans waged war without their aid. Their military technique relied heavily and bluntly on castles and cavalry which, when added to a deep religious faith, forged the essentials of their expansionist ideology.

Domesday Book may profitably be regarded as the antecedent of the agrarian survey which later became known as the 'Extent' whose form and substance were regulated by a statute of 1276, the <u>Extenta Manerii</u>. This contained 'Directions for making a Survey of a Manor' which really amounted to an inventory drawn up by 'true and sworn men'. Such Extents were made well into the sixteenth century. They constituted elaborate topographical descriptions of whole settlements sometimes extending in length to many pages of manuscript without a single map to illustrate them. It was not until the middle of the sixteenth century that a graphic expression of these topographical realities began to accompany written surveys; the English were late in realising that a picture paints a thousand words.

There is a further sense in which the locational aspect of Geography and Domesday come into conflict. From the account of the commissioning of the Survey written in the Anglo-Saxon Chronicle by a monk from Peterborough it is clear that the data were collected initially on a geographical basis.(2) England was divided into seven, possibly nine, circuits, one of which covered the South West of England, that is the counties of Cornwall, Devon, Somerset, Dorset and Wiltshire. That the shire formed the essential areal unit for the collection of the information is made explicit in the Chronicle, but the <u>Inquisitio Eliensis</u> goes further and confirms that its subdivision into Hundreds and then into actual manors also occurred;(3) it is this which brings the inquest closer to the actual soil, to those who farmed it and from whom the sworn evidence was extracted. Here then, one would expect the real landscape of medieval times to be recorded and the geography of it to be to the fore. It was not to be. The returns garnered on this geographical basis were laboriously and systematically re-arranged, one must assume at the scriptorium of Exeter Cathedral, for it is virtually certain that the Exeter Domesday is an initial conversion by some twelve clerks of the returns grouped by manors, boroughs and hundreds into a format in which the unit is the fief.(4) The only clear geographical entity which survived the rearrangement is the shire. Feudality took precedence over geography.

Nevertheless, if the English chronicler, prejudiced though he may have been, is to be believed something of the geography of the eleventh century may yet be reconstituted from the detailed nature of the enquiry he so poignantly recounts:

> So very narrowly did he have it investigated,
> that there was no single hide nor a yard of land,
> nor indeed (it is a shame to relate but it seemed
> no shame to him to do) one ox nor one cow nor one
> pig was there left out, and not put down in his
> record ....(5)

What credence should be given to this? May an answer in similar but whimsical terms be dared? In the otherwise not unusual description of the Cornish manor of Bodardle (fo.249b) in the parish of Lanlivery, a part of the Domesday Hundred of Tibestern, among the livestock ennumerated is one bull. This must have been quite an exceptional creature; it is the only bull recorded in the whole of Cornwall!

Indeed, it is the only bull to appear among the folios of the Exeter Domesday and the other Domesdays. Is this just a singular uncertainty or an omission?

When the literate and numerate aspects of geography are applied to Domesday, a kind of schizophrenia often emerges among the investigators. In the first place, there develops a feeling of awe and admiration for what after all is one of the oldest public records and probably the most remarkable surviving collection of quantitative data confined to a short time bracket for any area as large as a whole country in Western Europe. As folio after folio is turned no one can but be excited by the recurring entries for such items as population, ploughlands, ploughteams, pasture, meadow and such-like features of the farming scene. However, when this embarras de richesse is examined more closely inconsistencies, perplexities, difficulties and omissions abound. Some of these arise in the transcription of the text itself which is written in the highly specialised administrative language of the time. The Latin words themselves are not too difficult to read, but the highly contracted form in which they appear and the lack of consistency in the abbreviated forms used by the various medieval scribes in this their species of shorthand can present problems.(6) Even these difficulties are added to by the frequent absence of declension endings which can frustrate the elucidation of some subtle but vital point. Such problems associated with orthographic carelessness and inconsistency are considerably added to when, on the numerate side, it is realised that all the quantities are given in Roman and not Arabic numerals. Anyone who attempts the basic mathematical functions with Roman numerals quickly realises how prone to error the exercise can be and of course the Domesday clerks were only human and they made mistakes. When to all these difficulties our own uncertainties with regard to what was omitted are added, there is a need for caution; hence the reason for the title of this essay being The Geography of Exeter Domesday and not Domesday Geography. The two may not be the same thing and how close what is recorded in the Exeter Domesday comes to the realities of the eleventh-century landscape is a subject as intriguing as it is complex.

When in 1897, the distinguished scholar F. W. Maitland tried to look into the future of Domesday studies, he was moved to announce in the final paragraph of his Domesday Book and Beyond this prophetic thought:

> A century hence the student's materials will not
> be in the shape in which he finds them now. In
> the first place, the substance of Domesday Book
> will have been rearranged. Those villages and
> hundreds which the Norman clerks tore into shreds
> will have been reconstituted and pictured in
> maps, for many men from over all England will
> have come within King William's spell, will have
> bowed themselves to him and become that man's
> men.(7)

Many geographers have indeed come 'within King William's spell' and in the seven Domesday Geographies published in the years 1952-1977 have applied their numerical and cartographical skills so that the villages and hundreds have been reconstituted and pictured in maps.(8) Most of the recurring standard items such as assessment, ploughlands, ploughteams, population, values, woodland, meadow, pasture and livestock have been plotted on maps and many of them, using the hundred as the areal unit, have been expressed by means of densities per square mile. Of these recurring standard items, it may be assumed that the enumeration of the ploughlands and ploughteams would bring us near to agricultural reality and to the soil itself.

If Cornwall be taken as an example, ploughlands were systematically entered for most manors, but they were omitted in some instances and for those for which they are not, there are many problems of interpretation. For instance, the absence of any ploughlands for Trevell (fo.262) may perhaps be explained by the fact that the lone bordar on the manor had no arable land worth recording. All the land except one acre had been taken away from the priests at St Neots (fo. 207) by the Count of Mortain and this must have meant most, if not all, of the arable land, as the abstracted portion appearing under the Count's fief (fo.230) has ploughlands and ploughteams. Many of the other omissions may not so easily be explained away as those above; for example, the nine manors which were taken away from the church of St Petrock (fo.204b and 205). For them, no ploughlands are recorded, nor indeed are many of the other regularly-appearing items. In the complex manor of Winnianton (fo.99) with its collection of duplicate entries, the description for Trembraze (fo.99b), though stated as being unoccupied (<u>vacua</u>) is, nevertheless, credited with one ploughland. The parallel entry in the Count of Mortain's fief (fo.226) repeats the wasted nature of the manor but omits any reference to the ploughland. Another duplicate set of entries fares even worse. Folio 101 clearly records for Poundstock and St Gennys that 'twelve teams can plough the whole of the land of these two manors' but in folios 238 and 238b, where they are listed separately, they are credited with 6 and 10 ploughlands respectively. Ludgvan has a most interesting and curious anomaly in its ploughlands. The Domesday scribe, having written down at the end of folio 260 that 'fifteen teams can plough this' begins the next folio 260b with a correct repeat of the hidage but then states 'thirty teams can plough this'. In view of these uncertainties it is not possible to give a precise number of ploughlands in Cornwall, but it is about 2,562.

There has been considerable discussion as to the exact meaning of the term ploughland. Some scholars have regarded it as a statement of the number of ploughteams that were at work at the earlier time of 1066. Others have believed it to be an estimate of the potential arable land of a manor; yet others have seen in it a large conventional element.(9) There is very little evidence in Cornwall to support the first of these contentions as no hint is given that extensive areas had been wasted or gone out of cultivation since 1066 or that there was incomplete recovery after the lean years consequent upon the Conquest. Whether the ughland entry refers to conditions in 1066 or not, what is very apparent in Cornwall is the overall deficiency in ploughteams for the actual ploughlands. Are we to understand by this that the land was not being tilled to capacity and that the arable lands were capable of extension? If this is so then most of Cornwall must have been undertilled as there is only one example, Anthony (fo.181), where the ploughteams exceed the ploughlands and only fourteen entries in which they are the same. Various explanations have been attempted for this deficiency of ploughteams, none of which carries much conviction, not even the apparently most plausible one that the excess of ploughland over ploughteams represented the land which was lying fallow. If the manors where the teams exceed or equal the ploughlands are excluded the ratios between these items on those manors remaining show a very wide range and no clear indication of a two-field or three-field system emerges. In fact the range of ratios could just as well be suggestive of the in-field, out-field system or close variants of it.(10)

There is not much evidence, however, to support the third contention, namely that the ploughlands were purely conventional estimates. If ratios between ploughlands and other items are computed, they show a considerable variety and do not fall into ratio systems of a rigid and conventional kind. It is only in the ploughlands of the very large manors that one can detect a certain artificiality in the figures; thirty out of thirty-three manors with 20 ploughlands or more being in multiples of ten.

Although the Cornish entries for ploughteams are reasonably consistent and straightforward, they are not without uncertainties. The text nearly always makes the distinction between ploughteams on the demesne and those held by the villagers. A peculiar arrangement seems to have existed at Polroad (fo.204) where the usual formula is forsaken. No demesne land is recorded but there are villeins and bordars who apparently have no ploughteams, yet the Count who holds the land of St Petrock has 'one plough and one other plough'. Of more significance is the complete absence of ploughteams from about one fifth of the Cornish holdings, but almost all of these have ploughlands. Although most of these manors are inhabited, in only two cases are there more than six people recorded. It is tempting to speculate on the economy of such holdings for where no deficiency in the record is suspected it may well be that these farmers relied on hand tools in their small 'in-fields' or pursued a non-arable type of agriculture.

Some manors appear to possess ploughteams far beyond the capacities of their inhabitants to use them. The recorded population of Truthwall (fo.227) is one serf, nevertheless there is a ploughteam and other livestock besides, which is more than one man, even with the aid of his family could manage. The single-handed serf at Buttsbear (fo.244) and the lone bordar at Pigsdon (fo.397b) were in a similar position.

The total number of ploughteams in Cornwall was about 1,218 and this must be assessed in the context of 2,562 ploughlands. According to these estimates ploughteams amounted to only some 48 per cent of the ploughlands, the lowest for any of the south-western shires; the position in Devon, though somewhat better, is also strikingly deficient. Yet these two counties had not been devastated, as had the northern snires of England, nor is there any reason to believe that what the king's commissioners wrote down for Cornwall and Devon meant anything different from the ploughlands and ploughteams they accepted for the counties further east. Whether or not they carried out their inquisition as conscientiously as elsewhere, whether or not they understood the local folk or made their questions comprehensible to them, whether or not they were deliberately misled, or indeed whether the commissioners suffered from a peripheral-areas syndrome, one will never know. Had the margin of cultivation retreated over the previous twenty years? Were Cornwall and Devon stocked with ploughs to only a fraction of their capacities? These must remain open questions. With ploughlands and ploughteams one might have expected to approach the real landscape of the eleventh century but the reassuring first impressions gained from the apparently consistently recurring nature of the Domesday statements, on further investigation far from engendering confidence, bring to light all kinds of uncertainties.

Although the discussion has concentrated on the ploughlands and ploughteams, shortcomings and uncertainties in the literate/numerical approach can be instanced when the other data is investigated. It is clear that the assessment for geld was largely artificial in character and bore no constant relation to the other agricultural resources of a manor. Again the nature of some entries and the possibility of unrecognised duplicates make exact calculation most difficult. The most that any figures can do is to indicate the order of magnitude involved and in this respect Cornwall and Devon were very lightly assessed by comparison with counties to the east. With regard to population totals, owing to the nature of the Domesday entries, it is unlikely that two persons will sum the figures and reach identical totals; moreover the figures are of recorded population and presumably represent heads of households. By what factor should they be multiplied to obtain the actual population? Even then it is impossible to state how comprehensive were these Domesday statistics, as it does seem as if quite a number of people have been left unaccounted for. The ecclesiastical members of named institutions in Cornwall are not given, and there are twenty-six places which do not have any recorded inhabitants. Surprisingly also, for Cornwall there are no craftsmen mentioned, no salt-workers, no millers, not even a fisherman or a tinner! When investigation turns to the entries for woodland, pasture and meadow the problem to be overcome is that of the differing nature of the units of measure adopted. The amounts are expressed in terms of either acres or linear dimensions; the former cannot be related to modern uses of the term and the linear formula is obscure not only as regards the units of measurement employed but also the meaning of the formula itself. Means have been found to display the various data of Domesday Book on maps and doubtless they provide new ways of marshalling and expressing the information in a striking manner. Nevertheless cartographic techniques cannot make good the deficiencies and uncertainties in the data nor the imprecision of the arithmetic; at their best therefore, they can provide but a generalised picture without too high an expectation of their penetrating through the data to the geographical reality of eleventh-century South-West England. Moreover, the map symbols representing the data can only be placed on the identified, named manors, a subject which will be reopened and addressed later.

Attention may now be turned to that other focus of the Geographer, and the landscape approach be applied to the data of Domesday Book. A good example to demonstrate the effect of topography and to build up in the mind's eye the eleventh-century scene is provided by relating the Domesday data to the site and setting of Kilkhampton (fo.101). In north Cornwall at just over 500 feet in a valley-head stands the original nucleus of the village (SS253113). On its western and northern sides the map (Fig.1) indicates, extending downhill on the valley-sides, several small, now enclosed, fields which by the size and elongated shape of their hedgebanks irresistibly suggest that they are fossilized remnants of medieval so-called open-field or subdivided arable strip cultivation. Domesday Book confirms that the king held the manor, that there was arable land for forty ploughs and that in demesne the king had nine ploughs and the villagers twenty-six ploughs. To the east of the village, across the water divide, is an extensive area in the gently-sloping valley-head of the stream named Abbery Water into which this arrangement of hedgebanks does not penetrate. It did not do so when Joel Gascoyne mapped this area in the 1690s and neither did it when the Ordnance Survey produced its six-inch map in the 1880s; moreover, they printed across it 'Lord's Meadow'.(11) Domesday Book records the king as having thirty acres of meadow in this manor – the largest amount assigned to any one manor in the whole of Cornwall. For good measure, the west-flowing streams reach base-level from 500 feet in a short distance and are thus capable of substantial dissection; a steep-sided interfluvial spur between two of the streams provided an ideal site for a motte and bailey castle. The King really had something worth protecting hereabouts, the manor of Kilkhampton itself rendered yearly eighteen pounds – by weight! William wanted none of that debased coinage!

Most of the ideas introduced above are capable of development and spatial extension. For instance, medieval meadow, since it provided the hay crop, would be best suited to a location near to water courses and preferably on valley-floors where the grass would grow most luxuriantly. In Cornwall, extensive low-lying meadows are not of frequent occurrence and this is the reason why overall not a great deal of Domesday meadow is recorded; of that which is, over a half lies at high levels on the floors of wide, open valley-heads excavated but feebly in the sequence of planation surfaces for which the Cornish landscape is renowned, and some as at Worthyvale (fo.241) (SX108860) and Tredaule (fo.242b) (SX234811) the meadow is at heights of 750 feet and 650 feet respectively.

Another feature of Domesday Kilkhampton, the medieval field pattern, is capable of very considerable spatial extension. As in its case, cartographic and topographic recognition of strip-field boundaries

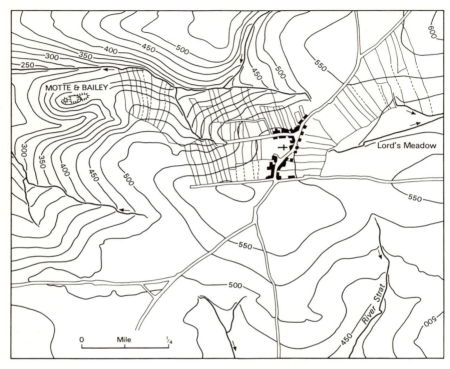

Fig. 1   Kilkhampton (SS 253113). Site, early settlement nucleus, and medieval field pattern.

and sets of enclosed fields with patterns reminiscent of strips are shown for both Cornwall and Devon in Figure 2. In spite of the known fact that many hedgebanks have been thrown down and the strip-field evidence ploughed out or built over, the map shows how widespread this form of field system must have been in both counties. In so far that this distribution map depicts only those strip patterns which have survived down to modern times, caution is required in its interpretation. It is but a partial reconstruction, there must have been many more strip patterns, but sufficient are there to indicate that sub-divided arable fields were formerly commonplace in South-West England even though the strict bureaucratic formulas of the Exeter Domesday give no hint of them, nor indeed, except for one solitary instance, does the Exchequer Domesday.(12)

To use and work the fields, the villeins, bordars, serfs and livestock had to be housed and there can be but little doubt that the Domesday Book formulas are really subsuming both in Cornwall and Devon the three main settlement forms – the single isolated farm, the small cluster of farmsteads or hamlet, and the nucleated village. Some entries can be referring only and obviously to the first of these settlement forms such, for example, as Speccott (fo.262) on a valley-side site at 360 feet in north Devon, with only one villein in its three ploughlands, or Trevell (fo.262) in the parish of Lewannick, Cornwall, where a lone bordar farmed. Examples of medieval peasant houses have been excavated in South-West England and one will not be far off what really appeared on the landscape in the above examples if a rectangular structure is imagined similar to but less sophisticated than the house which stood on a valley-side at 540 feet at Beere (SS689033). This farmstead was under two miles north-east of the large royal Domesday manor of North Tawton in the entry for which caput manor, its appurtenances may have been silently included.(13) The excavated foundations were of a three-room long house of single-room depth; in the middle was the living room with central hearth to the left of which was the sleeping room and on the other side of the cross-passage was the byre or shippon. A mixed economy was practised, as in addition to the byre, there was a barn adjacent and a corn-drying kiln.

The form of settlement next in size to the single farmstead presents something of a problem of definition. Most people recognise intuitively the difference between a hamlet and village but the actual line of demarcation among many variants can never be precise in all cases. It will not be far from the truth if one imagines the hamlet as a cluster of farmhouses and associated outbuildings usually grouped without any formal plan and without function in the administrative sense. A number of hamlet form of settlements has been excavated in recent years, albeit at high levels where abandonment has allowed exploration, for a reasonable picture to emerge. One such hamlet is at Hound Tor (SX745789) at 1,150 feet above sea level on an east-facing Dartmoor valley-side but the medieval fields lying adjacent to the hamlet extend above the 1,200 foot contour.(14) The settlement consisted, in its latest stage, of five long houses, two smaller houses and three barns with corn-drying kilns. The sequence of occupation at

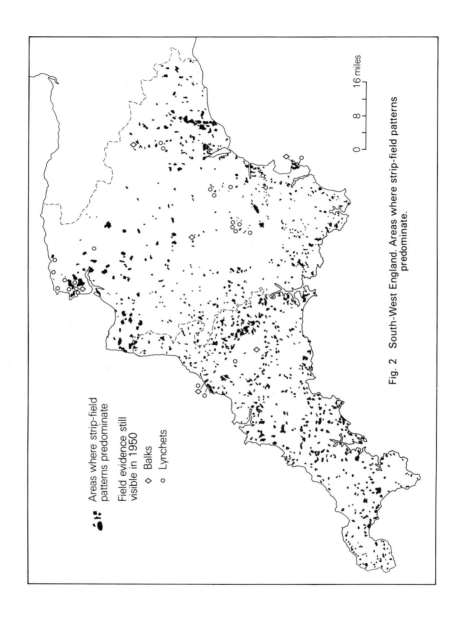

Areas where strip-field
patterns predominate

Field evidence still
visible in 1950
◇ Balks
○ Lynchets

0   8   16 miles

Fig. 2   South-West England. Areas where strip-field patterns
predominate.

this site began with small buildings and sunken floors, succeeded by turf-walled structures and then by houses with stone foundations and walls. Although the pottery found in the latter has been dated to the thirteenth century the sequence of earlier structures without pottery could take the period of occupation back to the eleventh century. In all probability this hamlet formed part of the Domesday manor of Hundatora (fo.103b). There is some evidence, admittedly emerging from documents somewhat later, that the hamlet with clusters of two to five houses would have been seen frequently in the landscape, even to have been the dominant form of settlement, in eleventh-century Cornwall and Devon.(15)

Buried deep in the shorthand formulas of Domesday Book lie the descriptions of true nucleated villages but in many cases they formed the caput manor and there is no means of knowing what proportion of the manorial population resided in the farms along the village streets or was dispersed in the outlying farms and hamlets. That the true village form existed in terms of size and function there can be no doubt. Many can be recognised located in relation to their medieval sub-divided fields, the frequency and ubiquity of which has been considered above; among these, examples in which the pattern of strips is developed over quite extensive areas are particularly noteworthy. What was revealed for the valley-head site at Kilkhampton is just as applicable to the spur sites at South Molton and Lydford and the valley-floor site at Croyde, all substantial manors in Domesday Book (Figs. 3, 4, and 5).

In the course of the discussion a number of comments has been made about the sites on which settlements have been built. If this aspect of Domesday is to be looked at more closely one needs a model of the landscape to refer to. The existence in Cornwall and Devon of a polycyclic landscape with planation surfaces is largely accepted. When such a concept is seen in the context of a westerly-tapering peninsula undergoing at the present time normal water erosion the valley systems and the landforms which exist between in the interfluves provide a variety of habitats for mankind. In the last resort the landscape can resolve itself into units of relief which are either 'flats' or 'slopes'. Although in nature no two of these units of relief will be exactly alike, the following broad categories of site are suggested as a useful model for reference: since the peninsula is so richly endowed with a varied littoral the first category may be designated coastal and then valley-floor, valley-slope, valley-head, spur and hill top. The other major landscape feature which must be given due weight is the height above sea-level at which the Domesday manors are to be found. Both aspects of the landscape are expressed in numerical form (Fig.6) and to make comparison possible both site categories and occurrence within each 50 foot contour interval are expressed in percentages.

A few comments are needed in the actual context of Domesday settlement. In the first place as far as the previous Celtic settlements are concerned the full range of sites was occupied and they extended over a similar altitudinal range to the later settlement. In truth, no significant differences or exclusiveness are being expressed

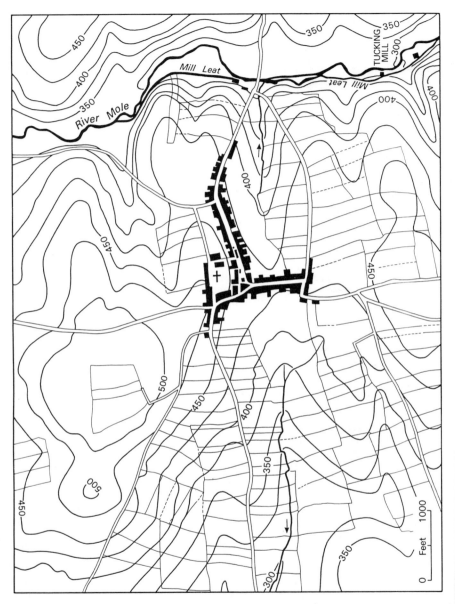

Fig. 3   South Molton (SS 714249). Site, early settlement nucleus, and
medieval field pattern.

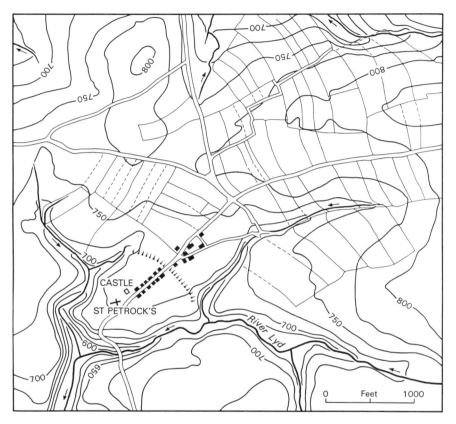

Fig. 4   Lydford (SX 509847). Site, early settlement nucleus, and medieval
pattern.

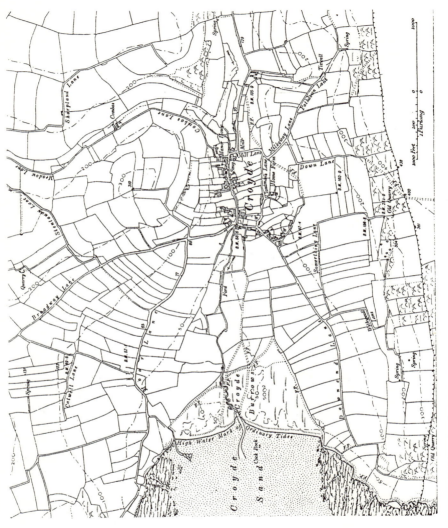

Fig. 5   Croyde (SS 446392). Early settlement nucleus on valley-floor site.

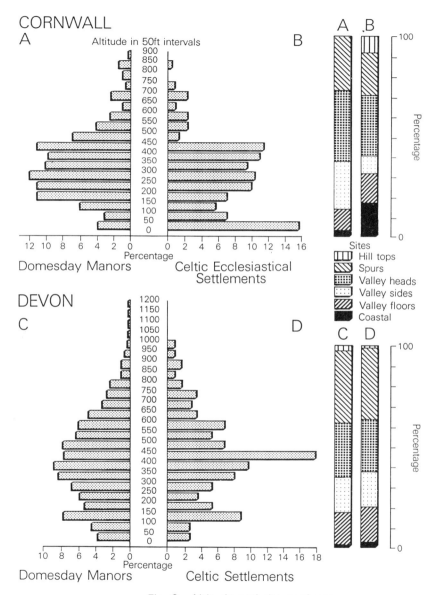

Fig. 6   Altitude and site analyses.

by these graphs as to the kinds of sites being chosen by the Celts and the English, nor, as was previously thought is there any indication that the Celts were primarily an upland-farming people. Domesday Book gives more than a hint of the colonising process: it makes unmistakeably clear the extensive expropriation of Celtic ecclesiastical properties in Cornwall by the Saxons, and later by the Normans. One could hardly expect the secular dwellings not to have suffered a similar fate and what holds good for Cornwall would certainly have applied to Devon at its earlier date of conquest and colonisation. The inescapable conclusion must be that farmers, be they Celt or Saxon, saw and interpreted landscape with eyes of similar vision and that there was no difference in the types of sites chosen by the two peoples, the Saxons taking over or settling alongside the Celtic folk, both in turn to be overlorded by the Normans; the fact that some 270 of the 330 Domesday manors of Cornwall have Cornish place-names but are held by Normans or Saxons speaks eloquently of the process.(16)

In Cornwall, not unexpectedly, only two Domesday manors were found on the exposed hilltops, a number too small to appear on the graph. A substantial number of manors occupies the spur type of site and the largest number of all is to be seen in valley-heads. There is no doubting the significance of the valley-head and spur sites as these two groups account for some 66 per cent of all Domesday manors of Cornwall. Not all that dissimilar are the values for Devon where 36 per cent of manors are on spurs, 27 per cent in valley-heads, 17 per cent on valley-sides, and 16 per cent on valley-floors. It must be stressed how very significant are the residual remnants of the interfluvial spur flats and the valley-heads below those flats in the siting of our early settlements and, since nearly all the Domesday places have continued in occupation, how significant these are in the present rural scene.

Equally revealing is the height range within which the Domesday manors are located. In Cornwall, a modest number of named manors lies between sea-level and 150 feet, while the landscape between 150 and 500 feet accounts for no less than three quarters of the total, but they continue above this altitude to heights of over 800 feet. On even a north-facing valley-side on Davidstow Moor at 870 feet stood Treslay (fo.240) (SX132886), where one Berner held the land which was farmed by three bordars with three ploughing oxen. In Devon even though the number of Domesday farms begins to fall off above the 800 foot contour line, some manors are found at quite surprising altitudes. High up in the head of a south-facing valley at 1,200 feet stands Natsworthy (SX722800) north of Widecombe where a certain Richard held the manor and, incidentally, grew grain, for there was 'land for two ploughs which are there'. Similar heights were being cultivated on Exmoor, where Lankcombe (SS771456) is found at 1,200 feet and, at about the same height formerly stood Radworthy (SS696428) in the south-facing valley-head of the River Bray. There Rainald had one plough on his demesne, the villeins had two ploughing oxen and there was pasture and meadow also. The occurrence of these manors at such high points in the landscape raises a number of important problems, not the least, of there being the necessity of cultivating such elevated land on the moorland fringes.(17) It is inconceivable that the 330 named places in Cornwall and the 983 in Devon absorbed all the land of lower and more attractive relief.

It is now appropriate to return to the problem of those settlements about which Domesday Book is silent. The majority of the place-names recorded are those of the demesne manors, the individual associated farms not being named. For example, it is not possible that Pawton (fo.199b), the largest of the Domesday manors in Cornwall with 44 hides and 86 recorded population and the only one mentioned in the Hundred of that name was the sole inhabited place, particularly when there is no evidence to suggest that there has ever been anything more than an episcopal barton on the site. A particularly notable example from Devon is another episcopal manor, that of Crediton, where the Bishop held a vast area extending over that fertile tongue of Permian rocks running westwards from the main outcrop. It is again not credible that a manor which had 185 ploughlands, an equal number of ploughteams, and 264 villeins out of a total recorded population of 407 consisted of the one settlement. Actually in the landscape there would have been the demesne and a village at Crediton itself and, separated from the caput, a number of hamlets and isolated farms. An arrangement such as this imposes severe limitations on the interpretation of the distribution map (Fig.7) since, by the absence of symbols, as around Crediton, the map suggests unwarranted areas of sparse settlement. To call attention to such examples and in an attempt to make the distribution of settlement more realistic those places with more than 25 ploughlands or 25 villeins have been indicated with large black dots. Even so it does appear as if the tip only of the problem is being mitigated by this cartographic device.

The deficiency of place-names has been considered since the time of Maitland and various estimates have been made of the total number of farms; a figure of 3,000 for Devon was suggested as long ago as the 1930s, but a more recent estimate by Professor Hoskins is that some 9,000-9,500 farms were actually to be seen in the landscape of eleventh-century Devon.(18) His figure is based on the frequent coincidence or near-coincidence of the number of ploughlands and villeins. On this assumption he argues that a farmstead should be allocated to every villein and that when the statement is made that so many ploughs can till the land of a manor there are that number of farms there in addition to the demesne farms. For Devon this would mean the number of farmsteads being of the order of 8,900 or 9,500 in round figures and for Cornwall the corresponding numbers would be 2,890 or 2,030. The existence of settlements in such numbers gains in credibility when related to the existence of farms at upland sites and the extent to which the moorland fringes were being exploited. Surely this points to considerable pressure on the available land which would be reflected in the degree to which the two counties were filled with settlements. Another indicator of the measure to which the landscape was farmed may be gleaned if the subject is viewed in the context of what emerged during the two centuries after Domesday Book. By 1350 the rural settlements in Cornwall were being served by some 37 places which had been designated boroughs or had markets. In Devon by the same date

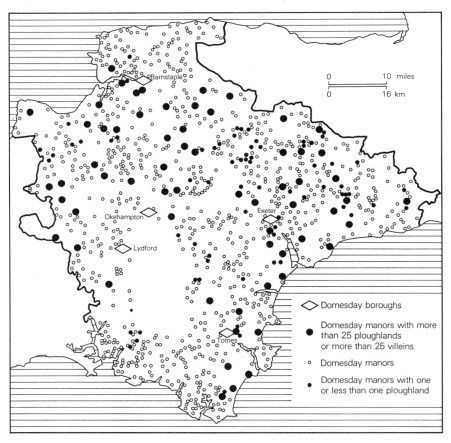

Fig. 7   The distribution of Domesday place-names in Devon.

76 places had been styled boroughs while a further 24 had markets.(20) Many of these places are named in Domesday and fall into the group of large manors. This is the logical outcome of the efforts of medieval landowners, who tried to enrich themselves by the foundation of boroughs and markets on their demesne manors; it also indicates how many demesne manors, in addition to becoming a focus for local tracks, possessed that degree of accessibility, which allowed them to extend their influence beyond the strict manorial bounds, so that they were able to function as nodes for a larger area.

It is very difficult to credit that so many centres for trade and exchange of goods would have been required were the landscape of farmsteads in eleventh-century Cornwall and Devon to be interpreted strictly and only in terms of the distribution of those places actually named in the Exeter Domesday. When the two south-western counties are compared with those to the east it is difficult not to sense that the friction of distance was taking its toll on the conscientiousness and vigour of the King's commissioners. It is thought that the inquisition had to be conducted in haste and completed to a set date. If time was running out and ardour waning for the commissioners on their journeys through Devon, it was even more so in Cornwall where the entries exhibit a lack of attention to detail. Even two centuries later, John de Grandisson, soon after his appointment in 1327 as Bishop to the diocese of Cornwall and Devon, in a letter to his friends at Avignon described how he was 'not only set down in the ends of the earth, but in the very end of the ends thereof.'(21) It would have been no less remote, probably more so, when the Exeter Domesday was in the making. 'Peripheral regions', it seems, are no new thing!

Notes

The author is much indebted to the Leverhulme Trust for its support in the preparation of this essay.

1. The Victoria County History of Cornwall, ii, part 8 (London, 1924) includes a translation of the Exeter text by Thomas Taylor (pp. 61-103) together with an introduction by L.F.Salzman (pp. 45-59). The Victoria County History of Devonshire, 1, (London, 1905) includes a translation of the Exeter text with an introduction by O.J.Reichel. The Exeter text, together with the Exchequer version, was also edited by a committee of the Devonshire Association, The Devonshire Domesday and Geld Inquest: Extensions, Translations and Indices (2 vols., Plymouth, 1884-1892).

2. Ed. D.Douglas and G.Greenaway, English Historical Γ   ⁺s 1042-1189 (London, 1981). Anglo-Saxon Chronicle, sub ₴ p.168.

3. *Inquisitio Eliensis*, Trinity College, Cambridge, MS 0.2.41. f.161.
    See also H.C.Darby, *Domesday England* (Cambridge, 1977), p.4 and
    Douglas and Greenaway, p.946.

4. R.Welldon Finn, 'The Exeter Domesday and its Construction',
    Bulletin of the John Rylands Library, 41 (1959), p.363. V.H.
    Galbraith, *The Making of Domesday Book* (Oxford, 1961), pp. 102–122.

5. Douglas and Greenaway, p.168.

6. *Domesday Re-bound* (H.M.S.O., London, 1954), pp.27–34.

7. F.W.Maitland, *Domesday Book and Beyond* (Cambridge University Press,
    1897), (reprint, London, 1960), p.596.

8. H.C.Darby, *Domesday England* (Cambridge, 1977). For titles, editors
    and contributors see Appendix 20, pp.373–374.

9. F.W.Maitland, *Domesday Book and Beyond* (Cambridge, 1897), p.425.
    H.P.R.Finberg, *Tavistock Abbey* (Cambridge, 1951), p.106.

10. N.J.G.Pounds, 'Lanhydrock Atlas', *Antiquity*, 19 (1945), p.71.
    R.Carew, *Survey of Cornwall* (London, 1602), p.19.

11. W.Ravenhill, 'Joel Gascoyne, a Pioneer of Large-Scale County
    Mapping', *Imago Mundi*, 26 (1972), pp.60–70.

12. Darby, p.95.

13. E.M.Jope and R.I.Threlfall, 'Excavation of a Medieval Settlement at
    Beere, North Tawton, Devon', *Medieval Archaeology*, 2 (1958), p.119.

14. E.M.Minter, 'Houndtor Down', *Med. Arch.*, 6–7 (1962–1963),
    pp.341–343 and 8 (1964), pp.282–285. Guy Beresford, 'Three
    Deserted Medieval Settlements on Dartmoor: a Report on the late
    E.Marie Minter's Excavations', *Med. Arch.*, 23 (1979), pp.98–158.
    D.Austin and M.J.C.Walker, 'A New Landscape Context for Houndtor',
    Med. Arch., 29 (1985), pp.147–152.

15. M.W.Beresford, 'Dispersed and Grouped Settlement in Medieval
    Cornwall', *Agricultural History Review*, 12 (1964), pp.13–28.

16. O.J.Padel, *Cornish Place-Name Elements* (English Place-Name Society,
    Nottingham, 1985).

17. D.Austin, R.H.Daggett and M.J.C.Walker, 'Farms and fields in
    Okehampton Park, Devon: the problems of studying medieval
    landscape', *Landscape History*, 2 (1980), pp.39–57.

18. W.G.Hoskins, 'The Highland Zone in Domesday Book', Chapter 2 of
    Provincial England (London, 1963), pp.15–52.

19. Andrew Fleming and Nicholas Ralph, 'Medieval Settlement and Land Use on Holne Moor, Dartmoor: the landscape evidence', Med. Arch., 26 (1982), pp.101-137.

20. M.W.Beresford and H.P.R.Finberg, English Medieval Boroughs (Newton Abbot, 1973), pp.76-83 and pp.86-101.

21. Edit. F.C.Hingeston-Randolph, Episcopal Registers of the Diocese of Exeter. John de Grandisson 1327-1369 (London, 1894), part I, pp.97-98.

The Church at Domesday

CHRISTOPHER HOLDSWORTH

Titles can sometimes be ambiguous, and so perhaps at the start I should make clear that this one does not portend a Last Judgement exercise upon the Church today. What I hope to achieve is an impression of the structure of the church at the time of the great Domesday inquiry. By *at*, rather than *in*, Domesday I mean to warn that in some senses Domesday is a very limited guide to a complete understanding of the church around 1086, one that needs rereading with care and supplementing with a number of other sources, both written and physical. Nonetheless the quantity and kind of information which Domesday provides raise many difficult problems, some of which have begun to be seen in different contexts recently. In one lecture I can do no more than indicate the main contours of the issues.

We may usefully concentrate by looking at the Domesday record for this county to discover what it does tell us, and what it does not, about the church. Within that record the obvious place to start is with the list of landholders within the county, which performs some of the same functions for the material that follows it as does a list of contents for a book.(1) There we find arranged roughly in the kind of order in which witnesses to a charter of the period might have been placed by a scribe, a number of names of individuals or of institutions which proclaim their churchly quality at once. The first is the bishop of Exeter who follows immediately behind the king. After the bishop come in unbroken succession the following entries: the bishop of Coutances, Glastonbury Church, Tavistock Church, Buckfast Church, Horton Church, Cranborne Church, Battle Church, St Mary's Church, Rouen, Mont St Michel Church, St Stephen's Church, Caen, Holy Trinity Church, Caen, and then among the final entries is the single name of Gerald the Chaplain. Altogether, twelve entries out of a total list of fifty-three landholders. These twelve must be supplemented by reference to three other individuals who appear in the main text under the rubric 'What the clergy hold from the king', but which, by oversight, was not included in the list of landholders which precedes the account for the shire.(2) These ecclesiastical holders fall fairly obviously into three uneven and dissimilar groups: quite on his own is the bishop, next are five very different clerics, and then a series of corporate bodies, all but one monastic. Let us begin by looking at them to get a general impression of what the entries within the Domesday record say about their position in 1086.

The bishop emerges as the third-wealthiest landowner within the county, coming after only the king and Baldwin the sheriff. He is credited with holding twenty-four manors, covering according to one calculation no less than 77,000 acres of land.(3) Behind this situation lay the careful work of the first two bishops who had centred their see on Exeter, Leofric and Osbern, who each husbanded their landed resources with skill, and added to the wealth of their see by their own benefactions.(4) Their work has to be deduced from the record of Domesday, but something else which had happened to the episcopal estate is obvious: already some lands had been divided up between the bishop and the community of canons who served the cathedral church. When one plots the distribution of the total estate across the county, something else leaps from the record: in the northern and western parts of the county, the bishop had little land whereas in the south-east and south he had more, but in no part of the county did he hold land in every hundred. Yet at this point we must remind ourselves that the whole episcopal estate was not contained within one county. Naturally enough for one whose responsibilities stretched to Land's End and the Scilly Isles beyond, he had extensive lands in Cornwall, amounting to eleven manors in addition to the twenty-four he had in Devon. But there were besides rich properties further afield, notably at Bampton in Oxfordshire and Bosham in Sussex, gifts made to the see by Leofric and Osbern respectively. The total effect of all his holdings made the bishop who directed the fourth-largest diocese in England the sixth-richest prelate.(5) This placed him on a par with a very small group of lay lords, those belonging to the top 42 families by wealth in Domesday England.(6) He well merited his position high in the list of landholders here.

What about the only other individuals of clerical character in the list, the bishop of Coutances, the men who held of the king in three places, and Gerald the Chaplain who merited a heading to himself? What have they to say about the church at Domesday? In one sense not perhaps as much as one might expect, since some, perhaps all, of them may have held land as reward for service to the king, and may not have exercised any priestly function in places where they held land. They could be temporary tenants who may tell us nothing about permanent institutions. Let us, however, look at them more closely.

Geoffrey of Mowbray, bishop of Coutances, was one of the inner circle around the Conqueror, who acted in many capacities to aid the duke-become-king.(7) In 1069, for example, he suppressed the rebellion of the south-western counties, and later he played a large part in the administration of justice, presiding over the famous so-called trial at Pennenden Heath. For these and other services rendered, he obtained a personal fee of enormous size, much of it in the south-west, which placed him among the eleven wealthiest people in the kingdom.(8) But he was celibate and so his estate did not pass to clerical descendants, but mostly passed on his death in 1093 to be added to the already-large holdings of Juhel of Totnes.

In comparison, the other individual clerics seem very small beer. The entries relating to them are however worth summarising, since they bring out the disparity in the resources enjoyed by individuals.(9) At South Molton, no less than four priests held a mere virgate (30 acres) worth twenty shillings in alms, i.e. they seem not to have paid tax. Saewin the priest held Swimbridge, as his uncle had done before him (one wonders whether the entry conceals a married priest?) which was taxed as for three virgates, and had various resources worth to their holder ten shillings. Braunton, held by Algar the priest, was a much richer plum, being assessed as one hide and being worth 50 shillings. Here it is not clear whether or not Algar had to pay tax, though the fact that he is said to hold 'in alms' from the king suggests that he did not. (10) Gerald the Chaplain is credited in the Survey with three manors which brought him an income of at least £3 a year, thus making him the second-wealthiest individual in this group, though poor in comparison with the bishop of Coutances. One presumes that whatever had been his work for the king it had been important, and one would presume that it was of a clerical kind, even though Exon places him among the French Men-at-Arms. This group of clergy appear as relatively privileged, holding more land than the typical priest across the whole country, who held, on average, around a virgate, which placed him at an economic level near to that of the average peasant.(11) Much more significant for us, however, are the corporate bodies which appear in the list of landholders for the county, and to them we now must turn.

They divide at a glance into two distinct groups, monasteries within the county, and monasteries without, this second division sub-dividing into English and Norman houses. Tavistock and Buckfast, like all the other English houses with holdings within the county, with the single exception of Battle, were creations of the so-called Tenth Century Reformation and its aftermath.(12) Tavistock was founded in about 974 when that movement, centred on the recreation of a stricter form of monastic life, was at full tide, whereas Buckfast, which began around 1031, came when enthusiasm had run down somewhat. They were endowed on a very different scale, Tavistock with lands and rights worth about £79 a year, and its younger fellow with only £17. (13) But both of them were poor compared with most of the pre-Conquest foundations in England. In the case of Tavistock, the record also shows us that the abbey had suffered noticeable losses of land to new Norman lords. Way had been taken by Baldwin the sheriff, whilst in Cornwall, Robert of Mortain, the Conqueror's half-brother and an energetic collector of church possessions, had got control of Tavistock land in at least four places.(14) Nonetheless it is interesting to realise that the income remaining to Tavistock was almost as great as that enjoyed by the poorest English bishopric, Chester.(15) When one looks at the placing of their lands in 1086, at least one fact of considerable significance for their futures leaps from the record.(16) Neither house enjoyed a compact estate, but held land widely scattered across the county. Each house, that is to say, would need to spend a good deal of time providing for the control and oversight of its lands. It was no doubt to make this easier that Tavistock, the house with much the larger estates, had in fact already by 1086 handed over part of its lands to tenants, but we must also recognise that pressure to do this came from another source, the need to find knights for the royal army, since Tavistock was one of the old-established monasteries which found itself after the Conquest with the added burden of providing knights for the king when he required. It is hard to discern the considerations which had led the abbot and his advisers to subinfeudate certain manors and not others — there is certainly little sign that, for example, the more distant estates from the abbey had been singled out.(17) But the point to be stressed here is that something like a third of the total holding had been granted out, in some cases to people whose connection with its military needs are crystal clear: Grento, a man-at-arms held Coffinwell, whilst Tavistock, itself part of the manor, was held by the men-at-arms.(18) In comparison with other English monasteries, Tavistock must have been under some strain to provide for its knights: elsewhere the proportion of land let out in fees to knights seems to have ranged between fifteen and thirty per cent, but Tavistock was not as hard hit as Peterborough, where Edmund King has calculated that forty-six per cent of the estate was subinfeudated.(19) Buckfast, with no such obligation to find knights, had no such people on its lands, and appears to have kept all its manors, however dispersed, at hand.

At this point one may usefully bring into discussion one very curious entry in the record: among the entries relating to the holdings of Ralph of Pomeroy, we find under Bruckland, a manor near Axmouth, that Aethelhard the monk held before 1066.(20) This was not a tiny estate since it was rated as one hide, although it was said only to be worth 12 pence. This introduces us to a practice which is very occasionally found in other parts of England. What appears to have happened is that individual monks who had inherited land were allowed to enjoy the use of it during their lifetime and to dispose of it by will. At the time this does not seem to have been considered to infringe monastic ideals. It certainly looks curious from a modern point of view, and seems to have disappeared with stricter ideas in the twelfth century.

With consideration of the holdings of English houses situated beyond the confines of the shire, we come across a very unevenly matched quartet. Glastonbury with a Domesday income of £828 was by far the wealthiest monastery in England, Cranborne and Horton, both in Dorset, were among the poorest, with incomes of £38 and £12 respectively.(21) Interestingly enough, however, Horton's four manors in Devon brought in about three-quarters of its total income, and so were of considerable significance to it.(22) Three of these manors were on, or near to, the coast, from Littleham (in Exmouth) at the west to Seaton and Beer in the east, though it also held Abbotskerswell which was separated from the other lands by two great estuaries. The other Dorset house, Cranborne, only had one Devon estate at Loosebeare in the parish of Zeal Monachorum, and the £3 which it got from the lands there was far less important to it than were Horton's Devon lands for it.(23)

Battle, the fourth English 'outsider' with lands in Devon, was a comparative newcomer on the scene, only having been founded by the Conqueror the year after his great victory at Hastings. To it William had given the church at Cullompton and a church in Exeter, which carried with it some property in Sherford and Kenbury in Exminster, the two together being worth under £5 a year. Battle had also acquired the church in Pinhoe, worth five shillings a year.(24) From these modest beginnings, within a year or so, Battle Abbey went on to establish a dependent priory dedicated to St Nicholas, on a site not far from the church which the king had given it.(25) A feature of these first gifts to the Sussex abbey which is worth underlining now is that they show how churches could be treated as any other property which might bring in useful income to their holders. In sum, monasteries based without Devon, but within England, enjoyed revenues totalling just over £21 a year.

In comparison, foreign houses overseas drew around £119, a sum over five times larger, reflecting the allegiance which the new king and his wife felt towards the institutions of which they had been patrons long before they came to England. Mont St Michel — that dramatic abbey on its tide-surrounded rock, overlooking both Normandy and its neighbour Brittany — as well as the two houses which William and his wife had founded in Caen, St Stephen's and Holy Trinity, all profited from the new resources available to Norman benefactors after the Conquest.(26) The cathedral church of Rouen, on the other hand, received the large manor of Ottery St Mary from King Edward in 1061, five years before his death. To it William added a manor at Rawbridge, near Axminster, a far less munificent gift, since Ottery was assessed at 25 hides, and said to have land for 46 ploughs, whereas William's grant paid tax merely as for 3 hides, and had land only for 12 ploughs.(27) But the point to be emphasised now is that Devon was typical in seeing a noticeable proportion of its wealth passing to foreign institutions in the era following the coming of the Normans, a process which in the church, as in the kingdom, preceded 1066.(28) Not that here, at least, the transfer was of land which had been long in the hands of the crown. Three of the manors given to Mont St Michel had belonged to members of the Godwin family formerly: Otterton to Gytha, Godwin's wife, and Dennington and Yarcombe to her son Harold, typically titled by the Domesday scribes as Earl Harold rather than King. As for the two houses in Caen, they received lands which had belonged to the great thane, Brictric son of Algar, whose estate went into the hands of the queen, and after her death in 1083 to those of her husband. It was not expensive to give away newly-gained lands.

Before we pass on to see what other sides of the church are illumined by Domesday, it is worth pausing to consider for a moment what the total picture so far revealed looks like, and whether the picture in Devon is typical of the country as a whole. We see a shire in which church institutions are well rooted in the soil. Altogether not quite a fifth of the land assessed for geld was in its hands, a proportion only slightly smaller than which it held over the whole country, or rather, over that part of the country covered by the Survey.(29) On the other hand, however, the proportion of church land held by the bishop – over a third – seems higher than in other shires, and relatively speaking not so much was held by local religious houses. It is striking too how great an inroad on local resources had been made by the religious foundations of Normandy, whose Domesday income, at £119 was a little larger than that enjoyed by all native monastic holders put together, £117. Conceivably these two features of the situation affected the future pattern of monastic foundation a good deal, since it was unlikely that anyone would attempt to establish a new house in close proximity to older ones, or to give it land in a village where another monastery, or the bishop, already held property. There may well be issues here which need explanation.

To find out more about the church at Domesday, we have to go further into the text and can no longer use the list of landholders as our starting point. Instead we have to look for references to churches within the holdings of the tenants-in-chief. The trawl proves to be a very modest one, but before asking why it is so small, it deserves a closer look.

There are only nine entries which unambiguously mention churches, and they relate to even fewer places, since three concern churches in one town, Exeter. We can slightly increase the total by adding in three references to groups of priests (single priests are less straight-forward), which brings the number of places up to ten. This gives us, in alphabetical order, Axminster, Colyton, Cullompton, Exeter (four references), Hartland (the entry mentions canons here), Kingskerswell, Pinhoe, Plympton St Mary, Woodbury and Yealmpton.(30) Nearly all these places were listed on terra regis, royal land, with the exceptions of Cullompton and three of the churches in Exeter. One of these was held by the abbot of Battle, another by the count of Mortain, and the last by the canons of St Mary's, a new foundation in the castle, who held of Baldwin the sheriff, their founder. One may note also that two of the churches elsewhere on royal land were actually in the hands of religious houses in 1086: Pinhoe being held by Battle and Woodbury by Mont St Michel. It would be hazardous to deduce too much from this evidence; it can scarcely have been the case that there were no churches in other villages where the king had land, but it probably is true that care was taken to list all those churches on royal land which were no longer in royal hands. Something else may be noted about the rural churches – thet all had various amounts of land attributed to them, ranging from as little as half a virgate (say 15 acres) to as much as the two hides (240 acres) enjoyed by the canons of Hartland and Plympton. This fact will not, of course, surprise any one who remembers that one of the purposes of Domesday was to reveal who held land; clearly royal officials would want to know about the land held by all kinds of churches, and about the incomes which may have fallen to those who owned them. But whilst one may suppose that the ownership of a rural church may usually have gone along with ownership of the estate which it served, the ownership of urban churches could have had a different explanation; that they had stayed in lay hands, or passed into the hands of a religious corporation like Battle Abbey, just because they were valuable pieces of property.

The most astonishing thing, however, about this list of churches is its shortness. It is surely inconceivable that in Devon around 1086 where Domesday list not far off a thousand settlements, only ten of them had churches.(31) We are therefore led to ask whether we can fill out the tale, and then to consider why the Domesday record is so peculiar.

Within the Domesday record itself, there is a variety of kinds of evidence which implies with different degrees of certainty that other churches existed around 1086. The fact that Juhel gave Follaton to the church of St Mary, i.e. to the church in Totnes which became a priory dependent on the monastery of St Serge, Angers, very soon after the Survey was made, makes it clear beyond doubt that there was a church in the town where Juhel built his castle.(32) Place-names which include an element meaning church seem also only to have one clear implication. There are two such names, Jacobescherche, i.e. St James church, Heavitree, and Aecclesia Sanctae Mariae, St Marychurch in Haytor Hundred.(33) With Instow, on the other hand, where a priest starts the short list of inhabitants (the other being 7 bordars and 3 slaves), one cannot be so sure that there was an actual church, since none is mentioned.(34) The priest may have been a domestic chaplain serving the needs of his master, almost certainly Walter de Claville, a considerable landowner. The three entries under the heading 'What the clergy hold from the king', as we have already suggested, may only refer to absentees, clerks who had received rewards for service to the king, but who did not reside on their estates, or to clerics who had actually settled in the places mentioned but who did not serve a church.(35) Only two priests are mentioned actually holding land from other men at the time of the Survey: Aelmer and Godwin. The former held Uplowman from Gotshelm, Walter de Claville's brother, as he had done before 1066, whilst the latter held Gidleigh from the count of Mortain.(36) One's doubts about whether these entries about single priests imply the existence of a church are increased when one notices that in six cases where named priests are said to have held certain places before 1066, they have been replaced by apparently lay tenants since.(37) It seems safer to treat this kind of entry with reserve, and not to add them into our list of places with churches. But one may note that even if one does count them in, it only brings the total number of churches in the county up to 25. The Geld Accounts in Exon increase the total, with references to priests at Exminster, Hollacombe and Newton Petrock, and to churches dedicated to St Mary at Modbury and Newton Tracey in the hundred of Ermington, and to St Peter at Plympton and Alentona in Plympton hundred.(38) These seem more likely to imply churches, like the references to more than one priest at places within the Survey, and so we can bring our total up to 20 places with churches. Beyond that I do not think that Domesday can take us.

The most obvious evidence which might help us to fill out this sparse total would be actual church buildings, but here too the tally so far is very small. The Taylors in their magisterial study of Anglo-Saxon architecture only listed Sidbury and St George's church in Exeter among churches which showed at least some fragments of Anglo-Saxon work.(39) Admittedly the problem of distinguishing clearly between styles in this period is a very subtle one, and it is abundantly clear that for the county as a whole the number of churches has not yet been altered substantially by examination of buildings. But we find another story if we turn for a moment to consider the results possible when literary-historical, spatial and archaeological insights are applied to the towns of the county. The recent very significant book on Anglo-Saxon Towns in Southern England, edited by Jeremy Haslam, gives strong reasons for concluding that Barnstaple, Kingsbridge, Kingsteignton, Lydford and Totnes (besides Plympton, for which we have already discussed Domesday evidence) had at least one church apiece. But it is for the county town that the results are most striking.(40)

Whereas Domesday only provides evidence for four churches, our local authors, John Allan, Christopher Henderson and Robert Higham, suggest that there were probably 29 churches and chapels within the city or within its suburbs by the end of the eleventh century.(41) Here I do not wish to put too much weight on the precise number, but to comment that this puts Exeter on a par, as far as numbers of churches go, with Canterbury, the ecclesiastical centre of the kingdom, and well above York, the northern capital.(42) According to a recent study (43), Norwich with 43 had rather more churches than Exeter in 1086 but the only other towns which have had larger numbers suggested for them so far are Winchester – over 44 – and London, which had over a hundred by 1200. There must have been no lack of churches for the Domesday population of the town. But how large was that population? Domesday gives us no count of burgesses but records that 399 houses paid rent to someone or other, mainly the king, and that there were 57 'wasted' houses (domus vastatae). From this figure it is usually reckoned that the city housed no more than about 2,000 people.(44) But it surely is reasonable to suppose that there were other houses too poor to have paid rent or to have enjoyed the other privileges of burgage tenure. It was presumably such considerations that persuaded James Campbell to leave his estimate of the size of Norwich as between 5 and 10,000, and I think we may allow a similar range for Exeter.(45) But even supposing that the population was nearer to 4,000 than to 2,000, the average congregation of the twenty or so churches can have been no larger than 200. We can see too that most of the churches in which they gathered were modest in size, and so we find here another example of the phenomenon to which Christopher Brooke drew attention some years ago, the very close relations which must have existed in many towns around this time between the priest and his congregation.(46) Small space forced them to know each other well, and it is conceivable that this knowledge was one factor which prevented unorthodox views from getting a hold here until well into the fourteenth century, although many towns of continental Europe saw many forms of heresy as early as the twelfth century.

Similar examination of all the kinds of evidence for rural churches within the county has not yet been undertaken. It would be a massive task, but as local studies proliferate it could be achieved. Now, however, we are left with two questions: why is the Domesday record so inadequate for rural churches, and is there anything significant about the group which it does mention?

The first thing to grasp is that in this respect Devon is not treated differently from a number of other counties; we are not faced with a particular case of 'up-country' misapprehension of the remote west.(47)   Many other shires have equally low figures for churches: Oxfordshire has nine, Cambridgeshire, five and Middlesex twenty, to take but three examples.   Most counties, indeed, are credited with under one hundred.   This situation has caused comment for a long time and some of the explanations have been frankly incredible.   It has been argued, for example, that there were actually more churches in the east of the country than in the west and that this reflected the break-up of the old mother-churches of the east with the severe effects of the Danes on the eastern parts of the country, and their replacement by churches in single villages.   This almost sounds as though a good dose of paganism produces a rash of churches.   How now is the situation explained?

In the first place it is realised that the process by which England was divided up into relatively small parishes took a long time. Something which had begun as early as the time of Bede did not finish until around the end of the twelfth century, although it probably was developing fastest between around 1000 and 1200.   It was associated with the break-up of large estates and the emergence of smaller village communities and may have taken place at rather different rates in different parts of the country.   But just as significant is the fact that the Domesday record was not directed at providing a register of local churches, but to discover the lands which belonged to the king and to other people, the value of all these estates to those who held them, and what the king could expect by way of geld.   It is noteworthy in this connection that the Ely account of the questions which the Domesday commissioners were to ask does not refer to churches.(48)   Faced nonetheless with a complex task which had to be undertaken very quickly, different groups of commissioners interpreted their task in different ways, there was not time for consultation with a peripatetic court, and it may well have been the case that they were affected too by the way that the local hundred juries presented the material to them.   In the case of Devon, it has long been accepted that the same commissioners worked here as went to Cornwall, Somerset and Dorset, and the record shows clearly that in all these counties very few churches were mentioned.   It is highly likely that what happened is that where a church had any value to its holder, it was included in the total value of the manor.   Something happened here on circuit scale which happened on William de Warenne's land in Norfolk where we are told that all the churches 'were valued with manors'.(49)   Thus the low number of churches has nothing to do with an actual low number of churches, but more to do with the way the commissioners worked here.   It is conceivable too that the process by which local worshipping places got resources allocated to the support of local priests was slower here, and this may have had some connection with the survival of an important group of churches which in some senses provided an intermediary level of provision between the bishop and the local rural community.   And it is to this area which we must finally turn.

No less than nine of the nineteen places where churches or groups of priests are recorded (this count excludes Exeter) seem to have supported institutions which are usually called minsters. As Christopher Brooke remarked four years ago, this is a term 'of marvellous ambiguity', since there 'is no kind of religious community or church bereft of religious community which was not at one time or another called a <u>monasterium</u>'.(50) Here we may, I think, follow M.J. Franklin, and use the translation 'minster' to designate a church which had in some sense pastoral responsibilities for an area wider than a single village. The study of minsters, or as they are sometimes called in the sources mother-churches, has developed a good deal in the very recent past. John Blair, in particular, in an essay in one of the many books on Domesday to appear in time for the main celebrations, has argued that one may expect to find a minster where a church is said in Domesday to be served by a number of priests, or where it is credited with a fairly substantial estate of one or two hides.(51) Occasionally other evidence may point in the same direction. Using these criteria he puts on a useful map of minster churches in England the following places in Devon: Axminster, Cullompton, Exminster, Hartland, Hollacombe, Modbury, Newton St Petrock, Plympton and Yealmpton.(52) There is not time to examine the evidence for these places in more detail, but two things are perhaps worth mentioning. The spread of places is much wider and more evenly distributed across the settled parts of the county than is the case for parish churches, monasteries proper, or episcopal land. If this pattern of minsters does represent a significant part of the institutions with which Devon was originally provided after the conquest by the Saxons, it does not make bad sense. Secondly, two of these minsters – Hartland and Plympton – were to have a continuing life as communities when they were transformed into houses for Augustinian canons in the twelfth century.(53) At Plympton, we know, the rump of the old group of secular canons were loath to accept the restraints implied by a tighter monastic discipline, so bishop Warelwast sent them off to serve out their lives attached to the church of Bosham which Osbern his predecessor had given to the see.(54) From that kind of episode it is perhaps easy to conclude that minsters were decaying at the time of Domesday; that now looks too simple a conclusion. They faded from the ecclesiastical scene as new styles of life came to be thought more appropriate for the clergy, and as more churches at a local level gained endowments and rights to run their own life with little continuing obligation towards the old minsters which had dominated church life earlier. There is much still to do to recover their true significance and to identify the buildings which housed them; Blair and Franklin are uncovering a seam which needs more work. With the minsters, however, we come to an end of our exploration of the church at Domesday through the pages of Domesday. Here, again, we find a feature of the church in the county which was not peculiar to it. Minsters are found all over Domesday England, though they stand out more sharply here, because thanks to the methods used by the commissioners on this circuit, very few local churches were noticed.

Notes

1. References to Domesday are given first to the Farley, Record Commission edition, and unless otherwise stated are all to the Exchequer Domesday in volume I. References follow the system used by Maitland, Stenton, Darby and others, i.e. by folio in the edition with 'b' after the number standing for the verso. For convenience, references to the Phillimore edition - Domesday Book, General Editor: John Morris, 9 Devon, ed. Caroline and Frank Thorn, 2 parts (Chichester, 1985) - follow in brackets, by chapter and section, so here, 100 (L).

2. 104 (13a.1-3).

3. W.G.Hoskins Devon (Newton Abbot, 1954 and 1972), 223, who here follows O.J.Reichel, 'The Devonshire Domesday. IV. The Domesday churches of Devon', Transactions of the Devonshire Association, 30 (1898), 279-80. One may have reservations about the way Reichel expresses hides in acres, but the relative scale of the situation stands. Domesday, 101b-102 (2.1-24).

4. Frank Barlow et al, Leofric of Exeter (Exeter, 1972), esp. Barlow's essay at 11-12. For Osbern and Bosham, see Frank Barlow, The English Church, 1000-1066 (2nd edn, London, 1979), 190-1.

5. Hoskins, 223.

6. W.J.Corbett, 'The development of the Duchy of Normandy and the Norman conquest of England', Cambridge Medieval History (Cambridge, 1926), V, 509-10.

7. See notes to Domesday (3).

8. David C. Douglas, William the Conqueror (London, 1964), 269.

9. Domesday, 104 (13a.1-3).

10. Reginald Lennard, Rural England, 1086-1135 (Oxford, 1959), 323 points out that 'in elemosina' did not always mean no payment was made.

11. Lennard, 306-32, on the economic position of the clergy.

12. Cf. Eric John in James Campbell ed., Anglo-Saxon England (Oxford, 1982), 181-91; and David Parsons ed., Tenth-Century Studies (London and Chichester, 1975).

13. David Knowles, The Monastic Order in England (2nd edn, Cambridge, 1963), 702-3, for monastic holdings in 1086.

14. H.P.R.Finberg, Tavistock Abbey (Newton Abbot, 1969), 8.

15. Corbett, 509.

16. Domesday, 103b (5.1-15), 103b-104 (6.1-13).

17. Finberg, 8.

18. Domesday 103b (5.13 and 5.1).

19. Cf. Edmund King, Peterborough Abbey 1086-1310 (Cambridge, 1973) 13-14.

20. Domesday, 114b (34.53). The holdings of individual monks are discussed in Barlow, English Church, 325, and by Knowles, 81 who had not noticed this example.

21. Knowles, 702-3.

22. Domesday 104 (7.1-4).

23. Domesday, 104 (8.1).

24. Domesday, 104, 100b, 100, 101 (9.1-2, 1.34, 1.4, 1.52).

25. David Knowles and R. Neville Hadcock, Medieval Religious Houses: England and Wales (2nd edn, London, 1971), 54.

26. Domesday, 104 (11.1-3, 12.1, 13.1).

27. Domesday, 104 (10.1-2).

28. Cf. Jacques Beauroy, 'La conquête cléricale de l'Angleterre', Cahiers de civilisation médiévale, 27 (1984), 35-48; D.J.A. Matthew, The Norman Monasteries and their English Possessions (Oxford, 1962).

29. Hoskins, 223; Corbett, 509-10.

30. Domesday, 100; 100b; 104; 101b, 104, 104b, 107; 117 (Stoke in Hartland); 100b; 101; 100b; 100b (1.11; 1.13; 9.1; 2.1, 9.2, 15.1, 16.89-91; 45.3; 1.12; 1.52; 1.17; 1.33; 1.18). Nearly all the entries are conveniently set out in H.C.Darby and R. Welldon Finn eds, The Domesday Geography of South-West England (Cambridge, 1967), 278-9.

31. Darby and Finn, 228: '... at least 983'.

32. Domesday 109b (17.58).

33. Domesday 118b, 101b and 105 (52.50, 2.8 and 15.42).

34. Domesday, 112b (24.26).

35. See above, pp.

36. Domesday, 112b; 104b (an entry not in Darby and Finn, possibly because only Exon says Godwin was a priest) (25.19; 15.7).

37. Domesday, Alric, 114b (Upottery), 116b (Stallenge), 116b (Huntsham); Doda, 107b (Dotton); Edward, 117b (Raddon); Goda, 117 (Abbots Bickington); Godman, 106b (Clannaborough), 107b (Bramford Speke); Wigot, 102 (Clyst St Mary); (34.50, 42.14, 42.23; 16.135; 51.6; 45.2; 16.51 and 129; 3.7).

38. Domesday, IV, fol.69, fol.65, fol.65b, fol.70bis, fol.70bis. Alentona is something of a puzzle, since other places with very similar names are not in Plympton Hundred: Alitone, East Allington (Stanborough Hundred), Alintona, South Allington (Coleridge Hundred). H.C.Darby and G.R.Versey, Domesday Gazeteer (Cambridge, 1975) do not list it.

39. H.M.Taylor and Joan Taylor, Anglo-Saxon Architecture (3 vols., Cambridge, 1965 and 1978). St George, Exeter, was added to Sidbury in the additional list in vol. 3. There is an important discussion on 'Anglo-Saxon architecture and the historian' by Simon Keynes as part of a survey of the post-Taylor situation in Anglo-Saxon England, ed. Peter Clemoes et al, 14 (1985), 293-305.

40. (Chichester, 1984): see the editor's chapter on 'The Towns of Devon', 249-83.

41. Anglo-Saxon Towns, 397-400: map, 399.

42. C.N.L.Brooke, 'The Missionary at home: the church in the towns', in The Mission of the Church and the Propagation of the Faith (Studies in Church History, 6, ed. G.J. Cuming, Cambridge, 1970), 66, 75. Cf. also James Campbell, 'The Church in Anglo-Saxon towns' in The Church in Town and Countryside (Studies in Church History, 16, ed. Derek Baker, Oxford, 1979), 119-35.

43. Alan Carter, 'The Anglo-Saxon origins of Norwich: the problems and approaches', Anglo-Saxon England, 7 (1978), 175-204 at 194-5 takes a more conservative view than Campbell, An Atlas of Historic Towns, ed. M.D.Lobel (London, 1974), Norwich section, 3, who has between 49 and 54 churches and chapels in 1086.

44. Domesday Geography, 247, 280-2; and Allan, Henderson and Higham in Anglo-Saxon Towns, 385.

45. Anglo-Saxon England, 174-5.

46. 'The Missionary at home', 77-9.

47. The phenomenon has often been discussed since William Page, 'Some remarks on the churches of the Domesday Survey', Archaeologia, 66 (1914-5), 61-103. O.J.Reichel, 'The Church and the hundreds in Devon', Trans.Devon.Assoc., 71 (1939), 331-42, criticised part of Page's theory but does not invalidate most of his observations. The best discussion is now in Richard Morris, The Church in British Archaeology (CBA Research Report, 47, 1983) 68-71 upon which the following two paragraphs are based. There is a fine overall view of the parish system in Barlow, English Church 100-1066, 183-208. See also the papers by Blair and Franklin below.

48. English Historical Documents, II, 1042-1189, ed. David C. Douglas, George W. Greenaway (London, 1953), 852.

49. R.Welldon Finn, An Introduction to Domesday Book (London, 1963), 196. The varied sizes of glebe are discussed most fully by Lennard, 306-32.

50. Quoted by M.J.Franklin, 'The Identification of Minsters in the Midlands', Anglo-Norman Studies, ed. R. Allen Brown, 7 (1985), 69. The whole article is suggestive and important.

51. 'Secular Minster Churches in Domesday Book' Domesday Book, a Reassessment, ed. Peter Sawyer (London, 1985), 104-42, at 105-6 where he lists in all six criteria.

52. Blair, 110 and 108. He seems to have slipped with Newton Ferrers (Ermington Hundred): the priests of Niuuetona who held of St Petrock's Bodmin, were surely in Newton St Petrock (Shebbear Hundred). The Domesday evidence can most readily be tracked in the Phillimore edition at 9.1; 1.4, 19.8 and 22.1; 45.3; 51.5; 51.16; 1.17; 1.18. For Axminster, see King Edward's grant of the minster 1060-1066 in Councils and Synods, I, ed. D.Whitelock, M. Brett and C.N.L.Brooke, Part 1 (Oxford, 1981), 557-9. For Modbury, see above, page

53. Knowles and Hadcock, 140, 143, 158-9, 170-1.

54. See above, note 4.

Domesday Devon

AUDREY ERSKINE & ROBERT HIGHAM

In conjunction with the delivery of the Domesday Commemoration lectures, in celebration of the nine-hundredth anniversary of the making of the Domesday survey, an exhibition entitled <u>Domesday Devon</u> was held in Exeter Cathedral Library from 14 to 30 October 1986. This was a particularly fitting location; for, as the Exon Domesday has always been preserved in Exeter Cathedral, this great manuscript could serve as a focus and basic <u>raison-d'être</u> of the exhibition in its traditional home. Moreover, the cathedral archives are comparatively rich in records which throw some light on what is, apart from Domesday itself, an otherwise sparsely-documented period, and these can be supplemented by documents from other archive collections in the locality. But documentary evidence can only be one aspect of an attempt to provide a glimpse of society and topography in this remote period; archaeological investigations and field studies were also drawn upon, though selectively, bringing them within the bounds of limited display space to illustrate local aspects of eleventh-century history. The exhibition was designed and executed by the authors together with Peter Thomas, Seán Goddard and Mike Rouillard.

THE GENERAL BACKGROUND

To set Domesday Devon in a wider context, the political and military background of the Norman Conquest was illustrated visually in excerpts from the Bayeux Tapestry. This 'strip-cartoon-style' contemporary Norman version of the causes and the progress of the invasion of England in 1066 shows the basis of the Conqueror's claim to the throne by his insistence that Harold was perjured and not the rightful king. For this reason, Domesday entries refer back to the reign of King Edward the Confessor and ignore the short reign of Harold. The embroidery (which it is, despite its popular title) most graphically illustrates the political events, as well as providing unique information on many contemporary details of costume, buildings and military practices.

THE DOMESDAY SURVEY

There are only three contemporary records of the Domesday survey assembled from the written and verbal evidence gathered in 1086. Two of these comprise what is generally understood to be the Domesday Book, that is, the Great and Little Domesday volumes among the public records, which provide the final text of the survey county by county. The third of them, known as the Exon Domesday, can be seen locally in the original because of its survival in Exeter Cathedral. It is the final draft of the assemblage and organisation of the return of information from most of the south-western counties - Cornwall and Somerset complete, most of Devon, about half of Dorset and a fragment of Wiltshire. The information in it is in fuller detail than appeared in its compressed and edited final form in Great Domesday; these are the only counties for which any earlier version has survived. Great Domesday has been produced in facsimile as part of the novocentenary celebrations, and it was possible to display a portion of this facsimile side by side with the original of Exon so that comparison of texts could be made. This elaborate reproduction is called the 'Penny' edition because it has a silver penny of the Conqueror included in its binding boards, which are fifteenth-century oak timbers and so have their origins in trees planted about the time of Domesday itself. Displayed beside Exon was the elegantly-produced and illuminated thirteenth-century Breviate (or summary) of Domesday from among the public records. It shows little sign of wear from regular use; it must have been produced for royal ceremonial or reference purposes, and is in itself an indication of the reverence displayed to the text of this great reference work two centuries after its compilation.

Reference was also made to Domesday for practical purposes in later times. It is interesting to note that Exon was not consulted when local information was sought, but the authority of Great Domesday was invoked. An example of the obtaining of a certified copy of the Domesday entry about Stoke Canon was shown. When needed by the Dean and Chapter of the cathedral, Bishop Stapledon acquired it for them from the public records in 1313 and similarly when the city authorities required a copy of the Exeter entries in Domesday in 1365, it was an elaborate royal exemplification under the Great Seal which was obtained.

Serious modern interest in the content and significance of Domesday began in the eighteenth century. The vast enterprise of publishing its text was first projected in Parliament in 1767, and the appearance of the edition of Domesday in 1783 made the text available in print to scholars for the first time. The Record Commissioners proceeded to a third volume containing Exon in 1816. The transcription of the text of Exon had been undertaken by Ralph Barnes, Exeter Cathedral's Chapter Clerk. His manuscript analysis was displayed together with the letter relating the remarkable restoration of a stray leaf of Exon in 1824, occasioned by the publication of the Record Commission volume. These were adjacent to a table of books relevant to modern study of the Exon Domesday text, of course centring on the 1816 edition but also including the nineteenth-century project of reproducing Domesday in county sections by the Ordnance Survey Office, by means of the process of photozincography (an interesting contrast to the new facsimile); and a selection of editions and studies of the Devon part of Domesday up to the present day.

THE DOMESDAY BACKGROUND

Before the twelfth century, the making and preservation of books and documents was largely in the hands of monks and clerks, and the transition from oral to written record was in any case a slow one. Surviving documents are few and most of them were concerned with the transactions of kings, bishops and monasteries. Those displayed aimed to supplement and further illustrate the local information contained in Domesday.

A. The literary background

Since the Cathedral Library was effectively founded before 1072 by Bishop Leofric's gift to his church of some sixty-six manuscript books, it was also possible to provide comment on an important aspect of the eleventh century not reflected in Domesday itself, the condition of culture and learning. The greatest literary treasure of the library, and sole survivor in situ of the orginal donation by Leofric, is the Exeter Book of Poetry, a collection of verse written in the late tenth century, though containing some material originating as early as the seventh century. It is therefore a monument in itself to the survival of Anglo-Saxon culture over the Conquest period. It contains numerous riddles - short verses requiring an answer - and the opening chosen for display typifies the attitude to books of the tenth-century 'golden age', for it describes the making of an illuminated manuscript book, to which the answer is the Bible. But the Exeter Book as it is now bound is also an important record source for late eleventh- and early twelfth-century Devon. Preliminary pages preceding the poems originate from a Gospel book (not now in Exeter, but also part of Leofric's donation) used as a repository for preserving memoranda of numerous manumissions of serfs, early religious gilds and other local legal documents, some of which were quoted elsewhere in the exhibition. Other books acquired soon after by the Cathedral Library show another aspect of the cultural background, the impact of Norman learning on England. This was well exemplified by the works of two successive archbishops of Canterbury. Archbishop Lanfranc (1070-89), former prior of Bec in Normandy and renowned for his scholarship throughout Europe, edited from an earlier continental version a collection of Papal decretals, to be copied and distributed among English churches to spread a better knowledge of the canon law, and the manuscript displayed was copied, perhaps in Exeter, about 1100. His successor, St Anselm (1093-1109), also from Bec and of equal reputation, was a more contemplative scholar, confident in the power of human reason to illuminate the Christian faith, whose most famous treatise Cur Deus homo? ('Why did God become man?') was shown in a near-contemporary copy, in a volume which also contains some other treatises by Lanfranc among others.

B. The royal diplomas

   Much contemporary documentation must have been available in the course of the making of the Domesday survey, though none of it except some taxation accounts bound in with Exon has survived. The earliest local documents to survive are a group of royal diplomas from the cathedral archives, a selection from which were displayed, providing information about ownership and even the detailed boundaries of estates which document the already-complex history of several places in Devon long before their entries in Domesday. The cathedral's foundation charter (1050) is a unique document of the creation of a new diocese at this period and of the enthronement of Leofric as the first bishop of Exeter. The two dioceses of Devon and Cornwall (both held by Leofric from 1046) were merged, and the seat of the bishop moved from the rural location of Crediton to the city of Exeter, where the minster church of Saint Peter already existed. Edward the Confessor and his queen, Edith, enthroned Leofric (who lived until 1072) and the ceremony was witnessed by an impressive group of magnates, both lay and ecclesiastical.

   Two other diplomas displayed refer to Stoke Canon, an estate whose ownership was the subject of some dispute. The minster clearly had an ancient claim to the estate, but the date of 670 given for one diploma is fictitious. Neither does the existing version of the document date from the time of King Aethelstan, whose grant it purported to record, but from a century later in the time of bishop Leofric. The other diploma, recording a grant of land at Church Stoke by King Cnut in 1031, shows that the cathedral had at some time lost the estate and explains the reason for the fabrication of the other diploma. Leofric's effort was clearly successful, since Stoke was recognised as a property of the bishop when Domesday Book was compiled.

   The diploma of King Edward the Martyr, dated 976, is a famous piece whose content has been used to illustrate an early detail of land ownership in Devon. It describes a grant of land called 'Hyples old land', whose boundaries can be identified with an area round Cheriton Bishop. The former owner's name is also reflected in the farm named Treable (containing the Celtic element trev), and it is interesting that the area covered by this diploma was excluded from the eighth-century royal grant of land for the foundation of the minster at Crediton. It may well be that the area had continued in Celtic ownership until the tenth century, perhaps the reign of Aethelstan, who expelled some of the remaining Celtic population from Devon.

   King Edward the Confessor's diploma of 1044 predates Leofric's appointment as a bishop. The king granted to his chaplain seven hides of land at Doflisc (West Dawlish and East Teignmouth). Subsequently Leofric, as bishop, granted land at Bampton (Oxfordshire) and Holcombe (East Teignmouth, within the area received earlier) to his canons at Exeter, and the gift was confirmed by royal diploma in 1069 by William the Conqueror. This diploma is a remarkable document, the latest known to use the diploma style of the Anglo-Saxon kings, without a seal and its main text in Latin and the description of the estate boundary in Old

English. It is the last feature in particular which gives these diplomas such wide interest. They are by no means simply abstract records of conveyance of land, but provide, through their place-name and boundary evidence, information for the reconstruction of contemporary land-holding and topography. They are an eminently suitable complement to the evidence of Domesday Book itself. The high value placed on such ancient records by the cathedral authorities was illustrated by an illuminated copy of the foundation charter entered in the fourteenth-century lectionary of the church (as an entry under Saint Edward the Confessor's date), as well as by a royal confirmation of King Henry VIII of several of the Saxon charters, decorated with the arms of the bishop of Exeter, Hugh Oldham (1505-19).

C. The bishops and their estates

Bishop Leofric (1050-72) had probably been a westcountryman by birth, but he was certainly reared on the continent in Lotharingia. He survived the purge of the old English bishops in 1070. He consolidated the estates of his church, and endowed it liberally from his own possessions, as illustrated by the Latin version of his gifts of estates on the preliminary leaves of the Exeter Book. His successor Osbern fitzOsbern (1072-1103), a member of an illustrious Norman family, had also been a royal chaplain. The Domesday survey was carried out during his episcopate. Among illustrations of his career displayed was his only surviving original act, which is in favour of St Nicholas' priory, under his seal, perhaps the earliest English episcopal seal extant. This document might well have been written by one of the scribes of Exon. William Warelwast (1107-36), the next bishop, had many links with the Domesday period, for he was a nephew of the Conqueror and had been his chaplain. The copy of a royal grant by Henry I (c.1107) in favour of the canons of the cathedral recites the numerous properties with which William I had presented him, and specifically mentions St Stephen's church in Exeter. His own grants of lands and privileges to Plympton priory made in 1133, sealed by his own beautiful episcopal seal, made an interesting comparison with that of Osbern.

Documents illustrative of the history of the cathedral church of Exeter again made reference to the generous gifts of Bishop Leofric. The church of Exeter regarded King Aethelstan (924-39) as its greatest benefactor and donor of most of its holy relics. The list of the cathedral's relics, in a late twelfth-century version, expressly claims that most of them were given by him. But when it was changed from a minster (or monastery) to being the seat of a bishop and hence a cathedral in the mid eleventh century, it had been denuded of property in the intervening period. When Leofric became bishop, he introduced regular canons in place of monks and, finding it virtually without books, vestments, plate or church furniture, he generously provided what was lacking. The long list of his gifts is set out in the Middle English version of his donations preserved among the cathedral archives, and it is impressively munificent, in view of his equal generosity in providing estates. In Domesday there is some distinction made between episcopal estates and those set aside for the support of the canons and by the twelfth century their endowment was further clarified by gifts of the churches of most of the estates and others by Bishop Robert in 1148. Some glimpses of names of members of the Chapter at the end of the eleventh century are to be found in memoranda relating to the dates of their deaths made in the margins of the contemporary Martyrology of the church. The brief chronicle of the church of Exeter in an illuminated fourteenth-century copy was also displayed; it is without much eleventh-century detail beyond the notes of the dates of deaths of kings and bishops, though it is of interest that it follows the Norman interpretation of the Conquest – Harold is described as an invader of the kingdom and perjured – and also contains an account of such an extraordinary thunderstorm and earthquake at Christmas 1080 that people thought God's Judgement Day had come.

D. Domesday churches

There is little direct evidence in Domesday about churches, other than Exeter cathedral, or about monastic foundations. The references to churches or chapels, though meagre and not by name, are concentrated on those of Exeter itself, and have been interpreted to indicate five: the cathedral, St Olave, St Stephen, St Sidwell and St Martin. Some scraps of evidence from later sources were gathered together to provide some additional details. There is a possibility that there were twenty-nine chapels (though perhaps from an interlineation only twelve) before the end of the eleventh century; and a grant dated c.1215, of twenty-eight pence to benefit twenty-eight chapels in Exeter was displayed to provide a definitive tally of the number in existence by the early thirteenth century. Concerning monasteries, some of the properties of the abbot of Tavistock are listed in Domesday, but little is said of other eleventh-century foundations. Therefore the remarkable near-contemporary memorandum concerning the endowment of Totnes priory as a gift to the continental monastery of St Sergius and St Bachus in Angers was shown as the outstanding survival of the documentation of a new foundation. It was made, probably soon after the time of the Domesday survey, by the great Breton magnate Juhel son of Alured, who was also responsible for the foundation of Barnstaple priory in the early twelfth century.

E. Other people and places

The deficiencies of Domesday in providing information about topography and society are hard to remedy from other contemporary sources, for it stands alone as a near-comprehensive record. But it certainly does not contain information about all the named places existing in 1086. A notable example in Devon is the omission of Dartmoor, whose name does not appear in records before the late twelfth century. An eleventh-century document from among the cathedral archives was displayed to remedy this. It gives the limits of a place called Peadingtun, a name not found elsewhere, but the bounds stated include

Ashburton, a good part of Widdecombe, Manaton and Ilsington, thus including a good deal of what we would count as Dartmoor today. Some other examples were also shown of the names of parts of Exeter referred to in later documents which must have been in use in the eleventh century, such as the 'red hill' – Rougemont in later times – upon which Exeter castle was built. Domesday rarely names people of less than substantial status. To provide some supporting illustration about individuals, the invaluable evidence from the preliminary leaves of the Exeter Book of Poetry was shown, providing names of people in Exeter and Devon of the late eleventh century not to be discovered from any other source.

THE TOPOGRAPHY OF DOMESDAY DEVON

Part of the exhibition was devoted to photographs and other items illustrating features of Devon's landscape at around the time of Domesday Book.

Exeter itself has been the subject in recent years of much research by the Exeter Museum Archaeological Field Unit. Included in the exhibition were materials illustrating the crafts and industries of the city, including evidence of textile production, leather-working, pottery manufacture and a selection of silver pennies of the reigns of Edward the Confessor and William the Conqueror. The results of excavations on the site of the Saxon minster (outside the west front of the present cathedral) provided a vivid reminder of the time of Bishop Leofric. Fragments of Romanesque architecture from the Norman cathedral, St Nicholas priory and other contemporary buildings completed this view of Saxo-Norman Exeter.

Landscape studies are frequently less precisely datable than manuscripts, and the remaining exhibits related to Devon in the eleventh and twelfth centuries generally. Some information was illustrated, mainly through photographs, on the following themes.

A. The countryside

The Devon landscape, like that of other westerly parts of Britain, is an ancient one. It was well developed by 1086, the majority of settlements already existing in some form or another, and the distribution of population reflected the variety of agricultural resources which are still apparent today. In 1086, it was largely a landscape of small enclosed fields, some perhaps of great antiquity, separated by lanes and banks some of which may still survive. Some of the boundary features described in Saxon can still be related to the present landscape, and some big hedgebanks which follow parish boundaries are likely to be Saxon in origin. Botanical study of Devon hedgerows by Max Hooper likewise has suggested a pre-Conquest date in certain cases. There were also developing at this time areas of open fields, of which Braunton Great Field is a famous survival, but these did not have the long-term impact which they did in the Midlands. By the thirteenth century, many Devon farmers were already enclosing these fields to make more convenient holdings. Much of the landscape of hedges and lanes we see today is probably the result of this work, which went on for several centuries.

Reconstructing the settlement pattern of 1086 is in fact very difficult, because Domesday Book describes not settlements but manors, that is, units of land tenure. Some small examples were little more than farmsteads, but others contained more numerous populations. The traditional belief, popularised by William Hoskins, in the Saxon origin of the nucleated village is now known to be misleading. Its widespread existence cannot be shown in Devon at this date, and even by the later Middle Ages, Devon was not a county of villages comparable with the midland landscape. William Hoskins also argued that in many areas — for example at Bowley, near Cadbury — the pattern of farms existing in the nineteenth century had hardly changed since 1086. Certainly there must be many farms more or less on the sites of their Domesday counterparts, though the earliest farmhouses to survive are later medieval in date. Emphasis on the farm may, however, have diverted attention from the hamlet, the cluster of farms which was quite probably the most common feature of the landscape. Maurice Beresford revealed through documentary studies the importance of the hamlet in medieval Cornwall, and Harold Fox has done the same for Devon, showing that some areas of isolated farms are the result of late medieval shrinkage of hamlets.

We are still, however, a long way from understanding the landscape of 1086. In such a large and varied county, settlement history would not have been uniform. A major problem is the extent of Dartmoor settlement at this time. Guy Beresford argued that the earliest occupation at Hound Tor, a hamlet deserted in the later Middle Ages, was Saxon in origin, but there is no real dating evidence and the idea has been seriously criticised on the basis of other fieldwork, especially by David Austin. In lowland Devon, one major problem lies in identifying deserted sites for archaeological study. Another lies in the analysis of the present-day settlement pattern (or that shown on nineteenth-century maps). It is too easy to assume 'continuity' even in an ancient landscape such as Devon. Hundreds of settlements still carry their Domesday name, but they may now look quite different. Cheriton Fitzpaine, for example, the 'tun with the church', probably comprised a hamlet cluster round the church in 1086. The street which provides its 'village' appearance is likely to have been a planned extension by a lord of the manor at a much later date.

B. Towns

In the Roman period, Exeter (Isca Dumnoniorum) was the only town in Devon, originally a legionary fortress and subsequently the administrative centre of the south west. In the following centuries, occupation in Exeter declined drastically. A monastery situated near the present cathedral is known to have existed since the seventh century onwards, but it was not until the late Saxon period that Exeter again became prominent in the region. During the reign of Alfred (871-99), fortified towns, or burhs, were developed to defend Wessex against the Vikings, and in the tenth century they developed as centres of marketing, minting and royal administration. The fortified burhs of Devon, which figure in a list compiled in Alfred's time, were Exeter, Barnstaple, Lydford and Totnes. It has recently been argued by Jeremy Haslam that there were also other 'proto-urban' centres in Devon at this time whose existence is not recorded. If there were, they had not developed significantly by the time of the Norman Conquest, for the boroughs of Devon in 1086 comprised only the four burhs, together with a new plantation at Okehampton established by a Norman lord in conjunction with his castle. Domesday Book also records a weekly market at Otterton, which scholars have not always taken into account, and there were presumably other rural markets too. Exeter by this time ranked as an important city; it paid tax to the king only when York, Winchester and London did so. It had nearly 400 houses and its perimeter was marked by the Roman walls and gates (no doubt with late Saxon repairs, though none has ever been identified), but its street pattern was largely different from that of Isca Dumnoniorum. Archaeological research by Christopher Henderson and John Allan suggests that most occupation lay along the east-west axis of the city and its northern parts. Totnes, Barnstaple and Lydford had simpler plans, laid out on sites with no Roman town beneath. The later decline of Lydford has left some of its Saxon lanes more or less intact, and its ramparts are still visible. It was the westernmost burh of Wessex. Barnstaple and Totnes were situated to defend estuaries, a common means of Viking attack. For Lydford and Barnstaple important archaeological evidence is as yet unpublished.

Okehampton was the earliest Devon example of a common phenomenon in England and Wales during the later eleventh, twelfth and thirteenth centuries. Planted towns were fostered by kings, lay barons, bishops and abbots in great numbers. This was a period of expanding economy and the founders hoped to augment their incomes from rents and market dues. Baldwin de Meules, sheriff of William the Conqueror, established a town at Okehampton, though by 1086 it had only a market and four burgesses. By the thirteenth century under the Courtenays, it had developed further. The planted towns of Devon (and Cornwall) were notable for their large number and small size, and were a fitting complement to a rural landscape comprised mainly of small settlements. Most of these Devon towns appear clearly only in the thirteenth century, but many existed long before they received a charter from their lord. Great Torrington, Bampton, Plympton and Tavistock were certainly developed during the twelfth century, the first three by lords of adjacent castles, the last by a powerful abbot.

C. Churches

Devon is not a county rich in remains of churches of the eleventh and twelfth centuries. The prosperity of the south west in the later Middle Ages brought widespread rebuilding which swept away most of the county's Romanesque architecture. We know that the Normans were active in building parish churches and establishing new monastic foundations, but relatively little survives in today's landscape. Even less survives of the churches which existed at the time of the Conquest. Documentary and place-name evidence demonstrates the existence of both rural and urban churches, but it is hard to visualise what they were like. The crypt beneath the parish church at Sidbury is probably late Saxon in date, and fragments of a church stand (re-erected) in South Street, Exeter. Outside the west front of the cathedral, part of the plan of Exeter's late Saxon minster church has been excavated by the Exeter Museum Archaeological Field Unit, through whose work Saxon and Norman fabric in St Martin's parish church has also been recently identified.

From the Norman period, there is more evidence. In Exeter, the two towers flanking the cathedral are the only major survivals of the Norman church (consecrated in 1133) which succeeded the Saxon minster. Almost castle-like in their proportions, they date from the mid twelfth century but have fifteenth-century details at their summits. Also in Exeter, the parish church of St Mary Arches contains fine twelfth-century nave arcades, and St Nicholas priory (an immediately post-Conquest foundation) has a Norman vaulted undercroft of the late eleventh century.

In the countryside, Romanesque architecture survives only in fragments. Later medieval builders frequently preserved details such as Norman fonts and doorways, both of which survive in great numbers. More Norman fabric probably exists in churches whose plans did not become fully developed with aisles, and western towers too probably contain early fabric. Frequently, however, the datable features such as windows and doorways are of later date. At Bickleigh Castle there survives a simple chapel with Norman nave and chancel. Despite its fifteenth-century details, it is a valuable reminder of the character of Devon's rural churches in the Norman period.

D. Castles

In many ways the castle epitomised the Norman Conquest. The fortified residences of William the Conqueror and his followers were the means by which England was subdued and the new aristocracy defended themselves. The Norman Conquest came to Devon in the spring of 1068, when William repressed a rebellion based in Exeter. This was the first of a series of uprisings based in towns, the repression of which, from 1068 to 1070, made the Conquest permanent. William himself chose the site of the castle at the highest point of the city, and then pressed on westwards to subdue Cornwall. A massively defended enclosure (the outer of whose two circuits has since disappeared) was built within the angle of the city walls. Its southern gateway (recently surveyed by Stuart Blaylock) still survives, among the earliest examples of Norman military architecture in England, yet contains some Saxon features.

We do not know how many castles were built in Devon immediately after the Conquest. There were numerous sites, such as Holwell (Parracombe) or Durpley (Shebbear), surviving only as earthworks, which were built either then or during the early twelfth century. But dating them precisely is impossible. The locations and circumstances of ownership of some, however, suggest an early date. The earlier of the two castles in the royal borough at Lydford was an enclosure in the corner of the settlement, like the castle at Exeter. Excavations by Peter Addyman produced evidence of timber buildings there. Totnes, Plympton and Barnstaple received large motte and bailey castles, a common form in this period. Totnes castle was built by Juhel, the Breton lord of south Devon, in the former burh which became the centre of his estates. Excavations by Stuart Rigold have revealed the foundations of a rectangular tower on top of its motte. Plympton was not established until the early twelfth century, and was the work of the de Redvers family, later earls of Devon. The origins of Barnstaple castle, excavated in the 1920s by Bruce Oliver, are obscure. It was referred to only from the early twelfth century, but may have existed from soon after the Conquest. Other castles, notably Bampton Castle and Great Torrington Castle, may also have had early origins, although their existence cannot be proved before the twelfth century.

The circumstances of castle foundations in Devon, which have been studied by Robert Higham, are complex. The situation of some castles may suggest that they were built, like Exeter Castle, during campaign. Burley Wood (Bridestowe) overlooks the road from west Devon to Cornwall and Blackdown Rings (Loddiswell) was built in an Iron Age fort in a high and commanding position in south Devon. In other cases, the castles emerged during the transference of landed power from the Saxon lords to their Norman successors, although the details of this process are obscure. The only Devon castle specifically mentioned in Domesday Book was Okehampton. Situated along the road from Exeter to Launceston, its site may have been chosen during William's 1068 campaign. By 1086, however, it was a fortified residence of Baldwin de Meules, sheriff of Devon and castellan of Exeter. Okehampton was his richest manor, and he himself held more land in Devon than any other Norman lord. Domesday Book's mention of the castle no doubt reflected the close association of the sheriff with the compilation of the record. Baldwin built a great motte on a rock outcrop, with a strong stone tower on its summit. His castle was an impressive symbol of the new Norman lordship, as well as a feature of the Devon landscape which had no precedent.

Selected Bibliography

J.P.Allan, C.G.Hen-
derson, R.A.Higham 'Saxon Exeter', in J. Haslam (ed.), Anglo-Saxon Towns of Southern England (Chichester, 1984).

D.Austin 'Dartmoor and the upland villages of the south-west of England', in D. Hooke (ed.), Medieval Villages (Oxford, 1985).

F.Barlow et al. Leofric of Exeter (Exeter, 1972).

G.Beresford 'Three deserted medieval settlements on Dartmoor', Medieval Archaeology, 23 (1979).

M.Beresford New Towns of the Middle Ages (London, 1967).

D.W.Blake 'Bishop William Warelwast', Transactions of the Devonshire Association, 104 (1972).

76

D.W.Blake	'Bishop Leofric', Trans.Devon.Assoc., 106 (1974).
P.Chaplais	'The authenticity of the royal Anglo-Saxon diplomas of Exeter', Bulletin of the Institute of Historical Research, 39 (1966).
H.Darby & R.Welldon Finn (eds)	The Domesday Geography of South-West England (Cambridge, 1967).
K. Edwards	The English Secular Cathedrals in the Middle Ages (2nd edn, Manchester & New York, 1967).
H.P.R.Finberg	'The open field in Devon', in W.G.Hoskins & H.P.R.Finberg, Devonshire Studies (London, 1952).
H.P.R.Finberg	'Hyple's Old Land', Lucerna (London, 1964).
H.P.R.Finberg	The Early Charters of Devon and Cornwall (Leicester, 1953).
H.S.A.Fox	'The chronology of enclosure and economic development in medieval Devon', Economic History Review, 28 (1975).
H.S.A.Fox	'Desertion and dwindling of dispersed settlements in a Devon parish', Medieval Village Research Group Annual Report (1983).
J.Haslam	'The towns of Devon', in Haslam, Anglo-Saxon Towns.
C.G.Henderson & P.T.Bidwell	'The Saxon minster at Exeter', in S.M.Pearce (ed.), The Early Church in Western Britain and Ireland. Studies presented to C.A. Ralegh Radford (BAR British Series 102, 1982).
R.A.Higham	'Castles in Devon', in Archaeology of the Devon Landscape (Exeter, 1980).
R.A.Higham	'Early castles in Devon', Château Gaillard, IX-X (1982).
M.Hooper et al	Hedges and Local History (London, 1971).
W.G.Hoskins	'The making of the agrarian landscape', in W.G.Hoskins & H.P.R.Finberg, Devonshire Studies.
W.G.Hoskins	'The Highland Zone in Domesday Book', in Provincial England (London, 1963).
C. Platt	Medieval England: a Social History and Archaeology from the Conquest to AD 1600 (London, 1978).
S.Rigold	'Recent Excavations at Totnes Castle' Trans.Devon.Assoc., 86 (1954).
F.Rose-Troup	Lost Chapels of Exeter (Exeter, 1923).

Acknowledgements

Grateful thanks are extended to:

The Friends of Exeter Cathedral and Exeter University for financial support.
The Public Record Office and Dr Geoffrey Martin for the loan of the Breviate of Domesday.
Editions Electo Ltd. and the Hon. Robert Erskine for the loan of the facsimile of Great Domesday.
Thames and Hudson Ltd. and Mr Neurath for the gift of photographs of the Bayeux Tapestry from their recent facsimile edition.
The Royal Albert Memorial Museum and Archaeological Field Unit, Exeter, and Mr John Allan and Mr Christopher Henderson for the loan of exhibits and display material.
The Devon Record Office and Mrs Margery Rowe for the loan of documents, display screens and much other invaluable assistance.
The Devon County Sites and Monuments Register (Property Department, Devon County Council) and Ms Frances Griffith for assistance in locating aerial photographs.
The National Monuments Register, University of Cambridge Committee for Aerial Photography, Cambridge University Press, The Society for Medieval Archaeology and Seán Goddard for provision of or permission to reproduce illustrative material.

Biographical Note

David Bates   studied at Exeter as an undergraduate and went on to take a doctorate under the supervision of Frank Barlow. He has been a Lecturer at University College, Cardiff, since 1973. He is the author of Normandy before 1066 and has just published A Bibliography of Domesday Book.

Frank Barlow   Fellow of the British Academy, is Professor Emeritus of Exeter University, where he was Professor and Head of the Department of History from 1953 to 1976. He has written many books on medieval history, including studies of Edward the Confessor, William Rufus and, most recently, Thomas Becket.

Audrey Erskine   is Lecturer in Palaeography and Archivist to the Dean and Chapter of Exeter. She has recently completed an edition of The Accounts of the Fabric of Exeter Cathedral, 1279-1373.

Robert Higham   studied History and Archaeology at Exeter, worked for a doctorate under Frank Barlow, and has been a Lecturer in the Department since 1975. He writes mainly on castles, which he also excavates. Recently, he wrote (with P.A. Barker) Hen Domen, Montgomery: a Timber Castle on the English-Welsh Border.

William Ravenhill   is Professor Emeritus of Exeter University, where he was Professor from 1969, and Head of the Department of Geography from 1971 to 1983. He has written widely on the history of cartography and historical geography, and was a contributor to the Domesday Geography of South-West England.

Christopher Holdsworth taught at University College, London, for many years and moved to Exeter as Professor of Medieval History in 1977. Since 1984, he has been Head of the Department of History and Archaeology. He writes on monastic history, and has edited the charters of Rufford Abbey.

EXETER STUDIES IN HISTORY

EXETER STUDIES IN HISTORY is a paperback series produced by the Department of History and Archaeology at the University of Exeter. Each issue is devoted to a major historical theme or problem, and makes available in accessible form the findings of the latest research. The series has won a wide readership in schools and universities and among readers with a general interest in history. Other titles in the series are:

ESH 13 Nazism 1919-45. Volume 3. Foreign Policy, War and Racial
Extermination, edited by Jeremy Noakes and Geoffrey Pridham
(forthcoming)

ESH 15 Intelligence and International Relations, 1900-45, edited by
Christopher Andrew and Jeremy Noakes (forthcoming)

For information on these and other titles in history and archaeology
produced by the University of Exeter, please write to the Publications
Office, Reed Hall, University of Exeter, Exeter EX4 4QJ.